Ways of Hearing

Edited by

SCOTT BURNHAM,
MARNA SELTZER &
DOROTHEA VON MOLTKE

Ways of Hearing: Reflections on Music in 26 Pieces

Princeton University Press
Princeton and Oxford

Published by Princeton University Press
41 William Street, Princeton, New Jersey 08540
99 Banbury Road, Oxford OX2 6JX

press.princeton.edu

Library of Congress Control Number 2021940611
First paperback printing, 2023
Paperback ISBN 978-0-691-23068-9
Cloth ISBN 978-0-691-20447-5
ISBN (e-book) 978-0-691-22597-5

British Library Cataloging-in-Publication Data is available

Editorial: Anne Savarese and James Collier
Production Editorial: Jill Harris
Text Design: Monograph / Matt Avery
Production: Erin Suydam
Publicity: Jodi Price and Amy Stewart
Copyeditor: Jodi Beder

Cover design by Chris Ferrante

This book has been composed in Harriet, designed by Jackson Cavanaugh, Okay Type

Contents

Introduction: A Convocation of Keen Spirits and Vivid Voices

SCOTT BURNHAM

When I last encountered my favorite great uncle, a warm soul who had always been the life of the party, he struggled to remember basic things and spent most of our visit unsuccessfully trying to tell a joke. Upon leaving, I began singing a German children's song that I knew he had learned in his youth. Suddenly he was right there, vivid as ever, singing along and even launching into another such song, with every word and every pitch in place.

Can we doubt that music enjoys a privileged access to our consciousness, often finding the resonance of our surest sense of identity? We are undivided from ourselves when listening to our favorite music. And this experience does not fade over time. Think how often you have chosen to hear the music that means the most to you, and remember those goosebumps—or those tears—that can arise with the very first notes. Or recall how hearing, say, a pop song from your adolescence not only opens up a world of memories but instantly recreates the entire emotional ambience of that time of your life. And now step out of yourself and think how we relish sharing music with others, how music offers a rewarding communal activity, in a church, on a dance floor, in a jazz club, a village square, or a concert hall.

Ways of Hearing addresses music in many of its individual and collective guises. It began as a way to commemorate the 125th anniversary of Princeton University Concerts, an organization long recognized as an innovative presenter of classical music performances. The book's curators, Marna Seltzer, Dorothea von Moltke, and myself, first encountered each other in the context of Princeton University Concerts: Marna is the Artistic Director of the concert series, while Dorothea and I are longtime members of a supporting committee. The initial idea was to commission essays by musicians and musical thinkers who would pay tribute to the experience of concert music. But we soon decided to extend the scope of the volume well beyond classical music, to include a greater variety of musics and a more broadly illustrious group of contributors. *Ways of Hearing* now includes musicians in bracingly different genres, poets, writers, scholars, an architect, a film director who is also a writer, a music critic, a dance critic, a visual artist, a physicist, and a Supreme Court Justice.

We challenged these remarkable souls to write about a specific piece of concert music, a quality or genre of music, or a way of being with music that has meant much to them. And we offered them the option of doing so through an interview, an essay, a poem, or even some sort of nonverbal creative expression. What we received has been extraordinary. As the contributors concentrate their attention on their chosen piece of music, or more broadly on the role of music in their life, they open themselves up to the reader.

When the novelist Richard Powers, for example, in the midst of his meditation on music's pride of place among the joys and griefs of his life, pauses and says, "But here's something I've never tried to tell anyone," we realize the depth of self that music has inspired him to reveal. It is likewise revelatory to experience the searching honesty of the musicians Jason Moran and Alicia Hall Moran, as they reflect together on how Alban Berg's setting of a Theodor Storm poem, as performed by Jessye Norman, sheds light on their own musical and personal collaborations, as well as those of far-flung poets, composers, and performers across the centuries. To listen in on violinist Arnold Steinhardt, known for his emotional nuance and complexity with the bow, as he thinks about Beethoven's *Grosse Fuge*—saying that "music is often beautiful and civilized, and this is not beautiful, and it's not civilized. . . . There's beauty in the world, but there's also torment and strife, and this is it"—is both to know that this piece is for our time and to know Steinhardt as an intellectually complex and nuanced interpreter. When the scholar and critic Daphne Brooks shows us how an "extended black feminist sonic monologue" composed and performed by the remarkable young singer Cécile McLorin Salvant can also be heard as a sonic analogue to the "loud dreaming" alive throughout the lifework of the late Toni Morrison, she opens up a vividly felt connection to one of the greatest voices of our age. To follow poet Nathaniel Mackey's improvisatory lyric is to find ourselves in the very mind of jazz. Or when Laurie Anderson and Edgar Choueiri together imagine protocols for a coming age of spatial music, we find ourselves on the horizon of a future in which music will be heard to gain exciting new dimensions. And when we learn that the first bench Justice Ruth Bader Ginsburg sat on was a piano bench, or that she has issued a definitive opinion on the sexiest duet in all of opera, we are all ears.

The music chosen by our contributors spans many epochs and cultures: from chamber music by Beethoven and Schubert to that of Messiaen, Reich, and Pärt; from vocal music by Handel to a song by Berg; from mainstream operas of the nineteenth century to an avant-garde opera from the late 1980s; from an anthem for a social movement to a captivating mix of bluegrass banjo and Chinese guzheng, feminist songs of Black sisterhood, and stirring jazz improvisations. The prevailing trends of this musical mix are revealing as well. As perennial giants of Western concert music, Bach and Beethoven get their usual share of attention, while jazz remains the essential record of a particularly African American genius. We take special note of the number of contributions addressing song and opera. Perhaps this is no surprise, given the human urge to merge language and music in so many striking ways.

These writings also teach us of the many roles music can play in lives well lived. We will encounter music as a spur to one's work and thought; as a social practice; as a form of storytelling; as a soundtrack for motherhood; as a gathering place for lost friends and role models; as the sound of identity, a potent form of loyalty to our better selves; as a form of courtship; as an indispensable means of healing and well-being; as electrifying self-discovery or the awakening of previously unsuspected selves; as a way to fill glorious spaces; as an inspiration for visual art; as a call to social change, or even to revolution; as a profoundly unsettling enigma; as a source of awe, joy, love. And we will learn what it feels like to perform classical music, jazz, and bluegrass, how it feels in the body, in the soul, and among friends.

The medium deployed in *Ways of Hearing* is almost exclusively language, with one stunning exception: the visual essay by Carrie Mae Weems, which exhorts us to "hear" in her images the lament that is also both a promise and a plea contained in the soul lyric by Sam Cooke: "It's been so long, it's been so long, a little too long / A change has gotta come." All the other contributions are expressed in prose, poetry, and dialogue. The usual claim that words cannot do justice to music has rarely stopped anyone and in fact stages the challenge met repeatedly in this book. Sometimes the writing itself becomes musical here, and not simply in the usual sense of rising to the lyrical: the poems, as well as some of the prose contributions, creatively enact techniques of voice that usually occur only in music, such as polyphony, counterpoint, and simultaneity. We will read and hear electric improvisations, probing interviews, dreamscapes, memories of great pain and great exaltation, rapt contemplations and embodiments, soul juxtaposed with soul, culture harmonized with culture.

These testimonies have been arranged in an attempt to distribute the different genres of presentation artfully throughout the volume, while also allowing thematic connections both obvious and subtle to resonate between immediate neighbors. Reading these contributions in order will thus impart something like the overall experience of a guided tour, while browsing in accordance with one's own predilections will create other journeys, other rewards.

We hope this book will be an inspiration to our readers, and even a source of joy: the joy of encountering other ways of hearing, of being with music; the joy of discovering new musics and thus new worlds. Our wager is that these essays, poems, and dialogues will, at the very least, encourage you to listen to the pieces of music they illuminate. You will find out "what we can learn to hear," as Richard Powers puts it in our opening essay. More broadly, these writings will familiarize you with the astonishing range of human interactions with music. As the opera singer Jamie Barton observes, "your experience is limited only by your imagination." So turn these pages and discover what happens when thoughtful and creative spirits reflect on the meaning and impact of their most treasured music. May your imagination grow with these ways of hearing.

Ways of Hearing

1 One, Two, Three . . . Infinity

RICHARD POWERS

I

My father wanted his own orchestra. He couldn't read music and his tastes tended toward the beer hall, but he loved singing and had a clear bass-baritone: "Blue Skies" at morning that changed, by night, to "Many Brave Hearts Are Asleep in the Deep." When he sang, our small house on the north side of Chicago turned bigger on the inside than it was on the out.

A junior high school principal, my father believed in giving his children the keys to every kingdom worth entering. We each played something: clarinet, French horn, guitar, viola. My instrument was the cello. The five of us would hold forth from different corners of the house, often at the same hour of the afternoon, in a riotous Midwestern nightmare out of Ives.

I remember, at nine, grinding away for what I was sure was hours—*This is, a sym-phony, that Schubert wrote and never fi-nished*—only to be stunned, when coming up for air, to discover that no more than fifteen minutes had passed. None of us loved practicing except my father. No matter how harsh the squeaks and clashes, he had his band.

The exhilarating monotony of practice was, for me, the paradox of childhood writ small. I lived between unbearable excitement and mind-crushing boredom. Those two states formed the twin poles of my days' endless question: *Is it tomorrow, yet?* Late one Sunday morning at the age of nine, I came to my father almost weeping from tedium and begged him to entertain me.

He told me to read a book. I said I'd read every book on my shelf. He went to the bookcase in his own room and picked out a small volume: *One, Two, Three... Infinity*, by the renowned physicist George Gamow. I opened it to a table of contents dense with adult type, grim and thrilling. But the biggest thrill of all was that my father thought I might be equal to this.

I struggled. But the first part of the book was called "Playing with Numbers," and I've always loved that thin edge between struggle and play. Page five had a drawing of a poor ancient Roman, taking forever to write out the number one million, which I could do in seven digits. A stunning idea formed in my head as if I myself had come up with it: however high a number anyone wrote down, I could write down one higher. The thought was intoxicating. Before long the book was claiming something far wilder, something that even now, more than half a century later, I still have trouble wrapping my head around: However large an infinite set I named, someone else could name one infinitely larger.

I do not remember the rest of that day, except that it passed in no time at all. My father filled my childhood with lessons, but never one larger than this: there were books that took you to places that never end.

My sons and daughters might have read, from my own sagging shelves, books by several other writers who credit Gamow's little book with starting their own careers. But I never had children, and my every house filled up each afternoon with a whole orchestra of instruments they never practiced.

My father died at 52, of cancer and drink, having outlived much of his life's best music. As I write this, I'm eight years older than he ever reached. Last year I began teaching myself to play piano. No matter how much longer I live, there will be an infinite number of pieces I'll never be able to play or even have time to listen to.

2

What I mostly did in life was fall in love. This happened early and often. "A pretty girl," my father liked to sing, "is like a melody." My first and formative love played the cello in a way that made me jealous of both her and the instrument. I lived eleven years with a pure, sturdy alto in large part because of how good we sounded when we harmonized. I once broke up with a statuesque model because she called the Beatles silly. For three years, I kept afloat on chaste correspondence built on mutual musical recommendations and disc discoveries. Late in life, when I met a woman who danced to Thomas Tallis while chopping vegetables, I knew it was time to get married.

I never cared what any of my mates listened to. I loved a woman who could not hear a shred of difference between Beethoven and cocktail-bar top forty. I loved a woman who could distinguish four different styles of bluegrass. I loved a woman in whose study hung a poster reading, "Beyoncé and I Will Handle This."

I used to audition potential partners under the guise of giving gifts. *Here. Do you know this one? Listen to* this. And their eyes, then, would be the best barometer for things to come. I needed only one little thing: for them to lean forward, like Mozart on his visit to Leipzig, shocked into fight-or-flight by the surprise motet of a legendary predecessor, his soul up in his ears, calling out, "What *is* this? Here at last is something one can learn from."

And many times in life, I got much more than that.

3

When my mother's operation for lung cancer came to nothing, the hospital still wanted to keep her. And they would have, if it hadn't been for my brother, the erstwhile French horn player-turned-surgeon. Instead, by miracle, we got her on a plane and across country to my sister, the guitarist, and her farm.

My mother's last bed looked west. She loved to lie still at dusk and watch as the deer came out of the woods to graze on the stubble in my sister's fields. On some days, that seemed like the whole point of everything she'd soldiered through in life up to then.

She, too, had had a good voice, and it stuns me now to remember how well she could play the organ, once upon a time. At sight-reading, she was especially good. But when we cleaned and emptied her townhouse after her death, it was clear that she hadn't touched her little Wurlitzer in a long time.

While my mother still lived, my wife and I made the daylong drive up to the farm as often as possible. In those months, we sat by as my mother, with unremitting cheer, tried to keep on breathing. She panicked at times, as any creature will when it starts to suffocate. But often her face was very much that of the young woman whose left hand, at those boozy parties that packed the small house on the north side of Chicago, sought out the chords for "The Sunny Side of the Street."

She had no special need for music at the end. The voices of people in the next room talking to one another as if time were nothing at all: that was the sound she needed.

My family and I were laughing over lunch when I went into her room to check on her. Her eyes were closed and her head tipped up toward the ceiling. Her face wore a look it had never known in life, an expression like the silence just past the last fermata of a good song.

Fast enough to shock me, the mortuary sent us a sealed urn that they said held her ashes. I weighed it in my hands, bobbed it a couple of inches in the air. Of course, the urn must also have held bits of ash from all kinds of strangers, maybe even acquaintances—countless people who wouldn't have minded sharing a little bit of my mother's urn.

We were free to spread the ashes anywhere we wanted. We brought them back out west, for a service where people she loved made the music she liked to sing along to.

∞

Reading, love, and death. Those have been my themes, through a life of writing. And music, the thing you're not supposed to try to write about.

But here's something I've never tried to tell anyone.

I liked to go to concerts alone. That way, I had no responsibility except to my own ears. Liking and not liking never mattered much, with me. What counted was what I could learn to hear.

I was twenty, in the middle of college. My first great love had come and gone and wouldn't reenter my life for decades. My father would die the following year. My mother would live another third of a century. I had no idea of the years ahead—the loves and deaths and stories I might make out of them. One weekday night, I went alone to a concert of solo violin music performed by an Eastern European virtuoso who, at the age when I was stumbling upon the fact that I could read my father's books, was already performing concerti with major symphony orchestras. I don't remember the entire program. I know only that it concluded with Bach's Partita in D Minor, BWV 1004.

The first four movements passed brilliantly enough. I'd grown up on Bach, and I knew that his touch could turn even a conventional dance suite into something deep and liberated. And I knew about chaconnes, the relentless, repeating variations above a short harmonic pattern or bass line. But nothing I knew or thought I knew prepared me for the Chaconne that ended the partita.

It began simply enough. The little theme emerged over four short measures. By the second variation, I realized that what sounded like eight chord changes in fact disguised the barest four-note bass line: a walk downward from *do* to *sol.* Nothing to it: the oldest trick in the book. Such romanescas were centuries old already when Bach was still in the cradle.

By the fourth variation, I could hear the gist. By the seventh, I sat forward on the edge of my chair, thinking, *Oh. Oh! Something's happening. We're going somewhere.* By himself, up on stage, the virtuoso wrestled with the theme. The twists he and Bach produced came in a steady stream, increasingly spacious, endlessly imaginative, built up from the barest building blocks.

Slow, sharp, languid, leaping: Each twist was shot through with its own distilled essence. Playfulness rubbed up against reticence, introspection lay next to full-out longing. I stopped counting and sat back, opened by the immense architecture rising in the air in front of me, under the fingers of a solo violinist.

Variations unfolded, one after the other after the other, inventive, elaborate versions of that tiny, four-note trip turning relentlessly back home. This was music built out of the smallest, simplest genes, assembled into endless forms too large to make out. I no longer knew what I was listening to, whether transpositions, diminutions, augmentations, counterpoint, fragmentation, displacement, or interpolation. What *I* heard was patience, sorrow, conviction, regret, grace, thanksgiving, delight in sheer dexterity, endurance turning slowly into a spacious *yes*, gameness in the face of restrictive pattern, and a nimble doubling down on that same determining scheme until crazed obeisance became its own escape.

A dozen variations rose up and disappeared. Then another dozen. The formulaic began to overflow into the unpredictable; the puppet got up and walked. Thirty variations in, and the massive minor of the piece brightened without warning into major, as if, at the lightest breeze, a hand swept aside the steely cloud cover and turned the sky ridiculous with blue.

The eternally recurring four-note descent grew obsessed with visiting every color on the emotional spectrum. In time, it returned to the minor, where it had begun. But somewhere in its sixty-four turns, the immense, passionate clockwork triggered something that, forty years on, I still can't explain. The light in the room dimmed and turned grainy. The floor of the auditorium fell away. Although the soloist wrestled on with yet one more intricate sequence of parallel structure, I drifted into the still spot at the center of spinning space. Time rose and fell like the planet breathing, leaving me aloft, floating on an upwell of pitches that, endlessly changing, held fixedly in place. All sense of my separateness dissolved in an ocean that rolled over everyone in the hall, everyone I'd known, everything I was or hoped to be.

I don't know how long I floated on that stillness. It astonished me, when the movement ended, to discover that the whole massive Chaconne had lasted only—only!—a bit more than fifteen minutes.

Years later I chanced on these words of Nietzsche, and that bottomless moment came back to me:

> Did you ever say yes to a single pleasure? Oh, friends, then you also said yes to all pain. All things are joined, entangled, smitten with one another.

I'm not a mystical person. This is the only life we get. I don't believe in the immortal soul, but for a moment outside of time, I knew what it felt like to have one. *Do, ti, la, sol.* Bach's Chaconne asks: *What can we make, here on this Earth, out of nothing at all?* And then it answers its own question: *Anything*. One, two, three, *four* . . . infinity. All that you've ever felt, all you have lived through—the sharpest excitement, the dullest boredom, the deepest grief, the softest joy—however much life gives you, there's more.

2 The Joy inside Sorrow

PICO IYER

Every November day, in our two-room apartment in Japan, as the sun rises over Mount Ikoma, casting golden stripes across our dinner table, my wife puts into our creaking boom box a CD of Handel arias. His high, ringing chords and notes of jubilation begin to echo around our home. Sometimes we put on Bach as well, or even Van Morrison, but it's Handel who feels to me like the laureate of the season: so often, he's bringing us a sense of slightly wistful celebration, a mix of rhapsody and sobriety, that seems to rhyme with the cloudless blue skies and the pinch of cold, the turning leaves outside.

Handel has been my unexpected companion, across several continents, for thirty years now. It feels strange to say that because if my friends were asked, they'd likely tell you that I listen to Jackson Browne and Joni Mitchell, to Springsteen and U2, and in recent times to my wife's beloved Green Day. My colleagues recall how close I was to a boyhood hero who became in time a boon companion, Leonard Cohen, whose liner notes I used to write. But my private joy, known only to my wife, perhaps, is George Frideric Handel, and in particular the choral music.

This is strange because I've never attended an opera, and have no real interest in arias as a whole. I feel abashed at times not to be a devotee of one of the accepted geniuses of the canon. When once I tried to learn more about my unmet friend, I heard only rather dismissive words about how much he wrote on commission and seemed a kind of Elton John of the eighteenth century, turning out coronation anthems on cue and seldom regarded as a composer truly listening to and channeling the music of the spheres.

Yet I think back to the long summer evenings of my English childhood: the rolling lawns, a stately home in the distance, the rare benefaction of light in a land so often dreary and sodden and chill. I think of the aesthetic that has called to me ever since I began commuting three times a year, from the age of nine, between my fifteenth-century boarding school near Windsor and my parents' home in hippie California. I longed for works that would bring the rigor of school together with the bright possibilities of my young adopted home. I've always been in flight from England, but I can no more get it out of my system than I can my earliest recollections; maybe it helps to hear from a longtime English resident who'd always seem a foreigner, and who could mix sentiment with an outsider's sense of order.

Or maybe it makes no sense at all to try to explain it away. I watch Lars von Trier's impenitent film *Antichrist*, and, during a shocking opening scene, am soothed by "Lascia ch'io pianga." I'm sluggish of a morning, and turn on "Tornami a vagheggiar." I go to the London museum celebrating the foreign rebel of my youth, Jimi Hendrix, and there—spirit of modern London!—I find a museum also consecrated to Handel.

Like most of us, I turn to music to reach the places that words find less accessible; even contemporary singers are unafraid of the very states of affirmation, the numinous, that writers increasingly shy away from. We more and more lack a Gospel spirit in prose; even those who dare to approach what cannot be spoken—Annie Dillard, say—have to use antic humor and irreverence to ground their flights. "Silly," they never stop reminding us, comes from the Old English word for "blessed."

I go to Sigur Rós concerts, therefore, to see what I cannot catch so easily on my bookshelves. Four figures silhouetted behind a screen, bodiless and invisible spirits giving voice to something far beyond them; there's a piercing high emotionalism in their lead singer Jónsi's voice that chimes with the otherworldliness (the Iceland) they're trying to evoke in all of us.

In the realm of popular music, Van Morrison can carry me up, up, up—"previous," to use his talismanic word—but by that very token, he snarls or throws out his songs like trash when the spirit fails to move him; the gruff and sunglassed figure onstage protects the candle inside him like a battlement. I like the respect he's paying to what's beyond our reach, the way he intones the same word again and again—much as Aretha Franklin used to do—so as to burst through the veil of words. Whether singing hymns or trying to invoke the "Sunday six-bells" and choral chants of his youth, he's always pointed toward the "ancient," which could be his word for what's hidden deep inside us. Every writer knows—in fact seeks out—that sense of surrender, and yet the impulse toward craft makes many of us recoil from the crack through which the light comes in.

Leonard Cohen—who brought that line to us from Rumi or Emerson or both—takes us deep, while worrying at theodicy and the words he cannot say like a theologian on the backstreets of Jerusalem. In person he was as gracious and open as Van Morrison was guarded. He had no secrets, he liked to suggest, and he didn't believe in either shortcuts or resolutions; he laid himself bare in every piece.

With Handel, though, I don't face the static of personality; I don't know who he was, or care. And what so moves me—literally transports me—is the way he blends ceremony with emotion. His pieces proceed like a courtier walking up a nave, yet they never can quite keep a smile or a skip out of them. Feeling slips out at the edges. Perhaps this is an Old World trick: to see how emotion becomes stronger the more it is contained; rhymed verse in a quatrain can bring more passion home to us, pressing against the edges of the line, than any free verse could.

Sometimes, in the autumn days in Japan, my wife and I would take my recently widowed mother-in-law, in her late eighties, on a drive along the Western Hills. She'd never had a car, so even a three-hour drive was a rush of exhilaration for the old lady, whose faculties were failing. We wheeled her out of her little nursing home cubicle, and into a tiny Toyota rented for six hours. Then we drove out to the Arashiyama Parkway, and as we watched the gold and scarlet leaves, under the radiant blue, what else could we listen to but Handel, not least his concerti grossi?

I'm not a religious person, but I've always noted that my friends who observe a religion have a solidity, a kindness, a sense of direction not always visible in the rest of us. All my life I've worked to try to mix hopefulness with realism: once by writing a book on the XIVth Dalai Lama, so practical and down-to-earth even as he never gives up on hope; once by coming at the same theme through the back door, with Graham Greene, undeluded observer of the modern world who never could turn his back entirely on faith. These days I try to put the radiance of the Japanese autumn together with the melancholy, in honor of the local precept that life is a matter of what some have called a "joyful participation in a world of sorrows."

Perhaps Handel is the meeting of those forces at some level deeper than the mind. He finds that place in me that will always rise to celebrations, and never want to forget that we have limits. Perhaps he is the voice of what I sometimes think is the point of life: to see autumn as the birth, as well as the obvious death, of spring.

In 2018, I, like many, tuned in to see the wedding of Prince Harry and Meghan Markle in a church just down the road, a fifteen-minute walk, from my old school. I'm not much moved by wedding ceremonies, but that opening clear sound, as the bride entered the holy space, of a single, silver voice summoning the heavens—a soprano singing Handel's "Eternal Source of Light Divine"—so pierced me that I could not stop thinking about it.

The next day, after I'd flown to Colorado, as I heard of an old friend's sudden death, I listened to the same piece again and again, on a trumpet played by Alison Balsom, then delivered once more by Elin Manahan Thomas. Then I turned to "Waft her, angels, through the skies." Then to "As steals the morn." It's now my morning service, the musical equivalent of *lectio divina*, that reminds me that there's something beyond what I see and know: each day as I awaken I turn on any of the Handel arias that speak of light creeping through the dark.

It's how I ground myself. It's how I return to a world outside of time. It's how I polish the silver and gold of my daybreaks. Of course I can turn to "Unto us a child is born" and other of his pieces if I long for jolts of energy. But such soulful, unhesitant, public expressions of what is deeply private feeling will always give me voice as not even the lines I've written here can do. It's not just Handel I'm listening to; it's everything that is deepest in me—and beyond me—for which I could never find the words.

3 *Fidelio's* Echo

GUSTAVO DUDAMEL

Why do we need to listen to Beethoven? In light of all the 250th anniversary celebrations of his birth, can we take a break at this point? The short answer is no. I believe that we will never tire of his music, and that we need the example of his spiritual strength more than ever. And I believe that his one and only opera, *Fidelio*, can show us the way forward better than anything else he composed.

The musical world celebrated the occasion of his anniversary with concerts documenting "Beethoven the Romantic" or "Beethoven the Revolutionary," performing cycles of his symphonies, concertos, sonatas, and chamber music. It is abundantly clear that he transformed the history of music, bringing it fully into the modern, postrevolutionary age, sounding values of individuality and universality that we continue to cherish. Yet above all, it is astonishing to recall that one of history's most popular and influential composers was, for over half his life, clinically deaf.

For most musicians, losing one's hearing would be a crushing blow. Indeed, Beethoven voiced the feelings of shame and alienation shared by many who are challenged by physical or developmental disadvantage in a letter he wrote to his brother in 1802:

> What a humiliation for me when someone standing next to me heard a flute in the distance and I heard nothing, or someone heard a shepherd singing and again I heard nothing. My misfortune is doubly painful to me because I am bound to be misunderstood; for me there can be no relaxation with my fellow men, no

> refined conversations, no mutual exchange of ideas. I must live almost alone, like one who has been banished; I can mix with society only as much as true necessity demands. If I approach near to people, a hot terror seizes upon me, and I fear being exposed to the danger that my condition might be noticed.

The tone is desolate; Beethoven alludes to ending his life. But in concluding this document, which would become known as the Heiligenstadt Testament, Beethoven would not resign himself to ruinous depression. "It seemed to me impossible," he wrote, "to leave the world until I had brought forth all that I felt was within me." In this ambivalent note, Beethoven bade farewell to his brother, then proceeded to compose the great "Eroica" Symphony, changing the history of music forever.

Has any composer before or since so powerfully wedded the personal with the universal? Through musical expression, Beethoven restored vigorous rhythm to the heart of symphonic music, and his fearless exploration of harmony, counterpoint, and musical form pushed the boundaries of all music that followed. In a sense, one could even say that it was precisely through his deafness that Beethoven was able to develop the creative and expressive tools that transformed the way the rest of us listen.

By our modern standards, Beethoven would almost certainly have been diagnosed as suffering from mental illness. Troubled though he was, he was in truth the opposite of a deranged genius: he was an artist of extraordinary spiritual strength and courage. He was possessed by a profound love of life and the highest aspirations for humanity, and his music expresses both those idealistic convictions and the intimate emotional challenges of his condition with compelling honesty. That sense of personal struggle, but ultimate triumph, is why Beethoven's music continues to touch and inspire billions of people around the world so profoundly to this day.

In Beethoven's immense oeuvre, there is no work more expressive of the overcoming of adversity than his only opera, *Fidelio*. The transcendent, transformative power of human expression is fundamental to my understanding of art, and *Fidelio* is the most vivid, compelling dramatization of that principle. Not only in its musical language but thematically and symbolically, the composer dramatizes aspects of his personal condition, connecting those struggles to universal themes.

The libretto is not a literary masterpiece, but it provided a template for Beethoven to "bring forth all that was within him" and challenge the human senses. Set in a prison, as the drama opens the characters are all trapped in their own limitations—they do not hear one another, nor do they truly see. It should in fact be quite obvious that Leonore (disguised as the male character Fidelio, in order to get into the prison and attempt to rescue her husband Florestan, who is a political prisoner) is not a man. But the rest of the characters are so caught up in their own political roles, drifting blindly in their own parallel spaces, that her imposture goes unnoticed. This sets the stage for a remarkable journey of persistence from darkness into light, or blindness into sight.

What could be a better symbol of darkness than a dungeon? Beethoven creates the terrifying darkness of his dungeon through the key of F minor. He used it again to make the same association in his overture to *Egmont*, Goethe's play about the Spanish Inquisition. So forbidding is the dungeon in *Fidelio*, that Beethoven has the timpani tuned in tritones, the interval known throughout the early history of Western music as the *diabolus in musica*, the devil in music. This tuning was a first in the history of orchestration, and it adds a chilling touch. When we first encounter Florestan, chained to the dungeon wall, he cries out: "Gott! welch' Dunkel hier!" ("O God! What darkness here!").

In a despairing recitative, Florestan sings of the horrid lifelessness that surrounds him. He resolves to put himself in God's hands and then begins to transcend his situation by writhing upward on the very word *Leiden* (suffering), as though pulling himself up by the bootstraps into the key of A-flat major, where he will sing his nostalgic aria "In des Lebens Frühlingstage" ("In the springtime of life"). At the end of this aria, Florestan undergoes a manically surreal hallucination in F major, in which the darkness lifts and a redeeming angel in the likeness of Leonore leads him to freedom. This amounts to a kind of seeing in the darkness, but it is not yet the true light of deliverance.

Another example of light breaking through the darkness occurs in the famous Prisoners' Chorus at the end of the first act. They are granted a brief reprieve from their cells and allowed to walk about in the sunlight. Heartened by this all-too-fleeting experience of the light of day, they too have a vision of a better future, as their words suggest: "Hope whispers softly in my ears! We shall be free, we shall find peace."

The opera is full of references to sight and to hearing. Even the sense of touch plays a part, as when Leonore first feels the cold air in the dungeon and shivers. For the characters of *Fidelio*, the senses of sight and hearing manifest themselves either in an impaired state or in a heightened, hallucinatory state, until the liberation of the prisoners at the end, which is also a liberation of the senses. This fraught emphasis on the senses relates closely to Beethoven's own condition, his terror of the sensory deprivation of deafness. The challenges so vividly overcome in *Fidelio* were *his* challenges.

Fidelio is also a work that features a great diversity of musical styles, partly buffo, partly tragic, ultimately heroic. One number in particular, the first-act quartet "Mir ist so wunderbar," has always struck me as one of the most sublime creations in all of music. The four characters find themselves in four different places emotionally, and yet together they create a stunningly beautiful harmony. What they share as vulnerable human beings transcends their emotional separation. Mahler clearly had this piece in his ears when he composed the slow movement of his Fourth Symphony, which opens in almost the exact same way—same key, same register, same pizzicato accompaniment—and shares the same transcendent tenderness.

The inwardness of this quartet reminds us that *Fidelio*, like Beethoven himself, symbolizes a bridge between the Enlightenment and Romantic eras. When the Minister of State Don Fernando arrives in the last act to remedy the injustice suffered by Florestan, he talks like Sarastro from *The Magic Flute*, namely, like the kind of enlightened leader that Beethoven admired. We know that Beethoven was fervently preoccupied with qualities of political leadership. His rejection of Napoleon Bonaparte as the dedicatee of his Third Symphony (after Napoleon crowned himself emperor in 1804) was a momentous act. It is inspiring to see on the title page of the autograph score how Beethoven obliterated the name of Napoleon, turning the "Bonaparte" Symphony with one brusque gesture into the "Eroica" Symphony. This biographical episode stands as an unforgettable mark of Beethoven's commitment to ideals of leadership that grew out of the Enlightenment. And yet the vulnerable tenderness of numbers such as "Mir ist so wunderbar" clearly speaks of the brave new world of Romantic subjectivity. And of course, the dramatic sweep of *Fidelio*—from struggle to triumph, darkness to light, imprisonment to freedom—replayed a celebrated trajectory in the Age of Revolution.

I cannot think of Beethoven in general, and of *Fidelio* in particular, without thinking about the spiritual father of my country, Simón Bolívar. Beethoven and Bolívar were two courageous, passionate visionaries, direct contemporaries whose parallel lives straddled the transition from the Enlightenment to the revolutionary Romantic era, who came of age in the shadow of Napoleon and went on to dominate the cultural consciousness of their time.

The message of liberty and struggle for freedom presented by Beethoven with such ferocious beauty resonates with the story of Bolívar, who faced colonial armies, survived political intrigues, and suffered personal tragedy, yet ultimately set millions of South Americans on the path to freedom.

As a Venezuelan and as a conductor, it is humbling and motivating to walk in the footsteps of both these giants. Just as Bolívar's words and deeds inspired men and women to strive for greater causes, Beethoven's *Fidelio* is a living, artistic proof of the power of human expression to transcend circumstance. And that, to me, is why *Fidelio* remains such a vital work: as a timely, impassioned case for humanity's highest ideals. And if ever we need to make that case, it is now, for we stand at another great crossroads of history, just as Beethoven and Bolívar did in the Age of Revolution. The choices we make now will affect the course of our collective welfare, and even the welfare of the planet itself. So may the relentless, striving idealism of Beethoven and Bolívar continue to create new echoes as we move into the future.

4 Beethoven Invents the Species Again

C. K. WILLIAMS

1.

Well here we are again waiting for Beethoven to kick-start the
species again to get us going again
on being wholly human we're anxious about it as usual the world
as usual driving us to distraction
we hatchlings who have to live here with our gulping muttering
selves fragmented just as we were

when we were half-beings whom music hadn't found yet it took so
long for music to find us remember?
back when we'd taught ourselves only to chip carve hammer spear-
points or blades while our psyches
kept burbling up blurred intimations of *more* we muddled mixtures
stricken with tongue-tied longing

but condemned to inhabit a recalcitrant world where tree was tree
hill hill earth soil lake etcetera
all *thing*-things entrenched in stony obstinate factness while we
kept wanting more more than fact
more even than what we could brain-glue together centaur
minotaur harpy please more more

we cried out always in pieces hoping for what we still couldn't speak
as again we hoisted our hatchets
but wait someone said wait Beethoven still says says again now
what of sound world-sound or wind

wolf sound or water might the way be in listening rather than
thinking or shaping even or praying?

2.

Not only Beethoven still says Mozart also and Bach and Schubert
Chopin Ella and Woody and Miles
and the rest we can trace all of them back because somewhere in us
we still hear that first hollow pipe
in a cave then Hermes devising the lyre and Orpheus tuning it up
and before we know it fiddle and harp

and bravo! the piano! finally Beethoven's piano listen again how
the notes amass then the chords
how the melodies climb the gentle cliffs out of their chords and
we're lifted once more to coherence
we and that ancient void in us brought together for this shining
time as music again fashions for us

this hallowed place where our doubts are lathed like dross from the
core of our now gentled fate
and where as we attend we're no longer half-things we once-
collages we're whole we who couldn't tell
if we were hawks humans horses we're complete now not hanging
out of the scabbard of matter

but caught by contained and spun from the music that embodies
those glad mysteries while we
in our rapture at being transformed again into musical selves as
one note one chord at a time we exist
as we knew all along thank you Beethoven thank you the rest we
should have and now once again do

This first edition of *Beethoven Invents the Species Again* was commissioned by Princeton University Concerts on the occasion of the collaboration between pianist Richard Goode and poet C. K. Williams, in a concert that took place Sunday, March 9, 2014, in Richardson Auditorium, Alexander Hall, Princeton University.

5 A Winter Drive

EDWARD DUSINBERRE

A low pizzicato note punctuates the opening chord of the Adagio, music that challenges my caffeinated frazzle on a frigid January morning as I reverse out of my driveway, on the way to the Takács Quartet studio at the University of Colorado in Boulder to rehearse Schubert's String Quintet. I have not played the piece for several years. Before I become caught up in the musical and technical details that dominate the rehearsal process, listening to this extraordinary slow movement provides an opportunity to reconsider its distinctive characteristics.

Admittedly, there would be more reverential ways to experience the Adagio than through a car stereo on my morning commute. Equipped with state-of-the art earbuds, watching the sun disappear behind the snow-dusted peaks of the Continental Divide in some scenic spot, I could perhaps create suitable conditions for an epiphany. But I am curious to experience the piece as it rubs up against more mundane conditions. The CD I listen to is our own Takács Quartet recording made in 2012 with second cellist Ralph Kirshbaum. Although the painting on its cover depicts a majestic snowcapped mountain viewed from afar by awestruck travelers, this morning the foothills west of Boulder are obscured by mist: if an otherworldly listening experience is improbable, perhaps other aspects of the Adagio will emerge.

A backhoe is blocking the street. There is a sign to PROCEED SLOWLY, but only a child on a scooter could find a way through the jumble of red cones that surround a small pit, dug to repair a gas leak or unleash the latest flood of cable entertainment on the neighborhood. I rev my engine, drowning out Schubert and drawing the attention of a worker, who glances indifferently in my direction before reversing the sign: STOP. A detour will add precious minutes to my journey time. I set off in the opposite direction while Schubert's chords proceed slowly, impervious to the profanities of a fractious driver.

The second cello's pizzicati continue in the form of a two- (or occasionally three-) note rhythm that lands with mesmerizing regularity on the first and third beats of every bar for the first five minutes of the movement. These pizzicati provide a frame while the first cello joins second violin and viola to become an additional inner voice. To create a balanced blend of sound, my quartet colleagues unify their bow speeds and vibrato, playing pianissimo as they provide a slow-moving chordal backdrop to a dialogue between the second cello and first violin. *Really, a backdrop??* I hear them protesting. Well might they bridle at a first violinist's glib characterization of their parts, marked *espressivo.* Sigmund Nissel, second violinist of the Amadeus Quartet, once offered a tongue-in-cheek description of a string quartet as a fine wine: the cellist may be the bottle, the first violin the label, but it is the inner voices that provide the actual wine. The idea is a good counter to any talk of a "backdrop," and appropriate with minor adaptation for this opening of the Quintet's Adagio.

But what about that first violinist? I have more often thought of myself as the cork than the bottle—at fault when the wine smells off. Throughout his chamber music Schubert writes exposed and treacherous passages for the first violin that can exude a pungent odor. However, his unreasonable demands are all forgiven in light of my assignment in this one Adagio. The first violin adds an element of fantasy to the opening: notes that question and speculate, seemingly improvised on the spur of the moment. While the second cello continues its pizzicato frame and the inner voices journey through their chord changes, I am propelled to the second and fourth beats of each bar by a simple dotted rhythm. When grace notes are added they provide the impetus to reach upward—a fourth, a second, an octave, a third or a sixth—before the higher note gives way to the starting pitch. As the distance of the intervallic leaps increases and the dynamic develops from pianissimo to forte, these gestures plead with the chords and the more objective downbeat pizzicati of the second cello, encouraging a heightened expressivity. At the ends of cadences my role is more reactive, acquiescing to the chord changes as I fall downward through the same notes laid out beneath me.

The hypnotic repetition of the second cello's rhythm contrasts with the commonplace actions I observe around me. In the rearview mirror a woman contorts her head up and to the left as she fastens a determined jaw around a large breakfast sandwich, her other hand juggling steering wheel and iPhone. Meanwhile, a shocking bumper sticker has just overtaken me on the left. *Jesus loves you but everyone else thinks you're an asshole.* A salutary reminder before a string quartet rehearsal: when one works so intensively with the same three people, one's tics are more irksome for being predictable. There is the thinly veiled criticism framed as an innocuous question, *Do you think that maybe . . .*, or that habit I have of repeating a self-evident statement in a slightly different way, as if it were too complex to be fully appreciated the first time around—indeed too sophisticated to be instantly comprehended.

In just a few weeks water will cascade down the gulley adjacent to the road, but today the creek is covered by a thin crust of ice. Commuters advance in slow motion, exhibiting varying degrees of impatience and resignation. At an intersection a postman hoots his horn at the hapless driver whose wheels spin in the slush. The chords of the opening phrase return and the first violin abandons its lyrical fantasy, now responding to the second cello's pizzicati in kind. When the second cello is seated opposite the first violin onstage, their pizzicati answer each other across chords that emerge from the middle of the group. The austere effect is reinforced by a further drop in dynamic in the chords: now *pp* becomes *ppp* and there is no *espressivo* instruction to encourage bowing arms. The change is one of both dynamic and timbre of sound. By using no vibrato, the inner voices can produce a bleaker sound, a sense of the music being stripped down, individual impulses minimized. In concert the slow repetitive arm motion necessary to execute the pizzicati produces in me a strange, trance-like sensation, as if from afar Schubert were operating my arm with invisible strings.

After just a few bars, I can no longer sustain the restrictive symmetry of the pizzicati, and reintroduce my dotted rhythm and intervallic leaps upward, alternating these with increasingly desperate pizzicati—desperate because as the music grows in volume and the second cellist pulls a cavernous sound from his instrument, I am incapable of matching his resonance in this higher register. When we performed this piece with cellist Lynn Harrell opposite me, he sat in the pause between the first and second movements sucking his thumb—a discreet way to soften his skin in preparation for these pizzicati. Dry skin would produce an unsuitably brittle sound. During concert performances I hope the exaggerated follow-through of my arm will launch my bony-fingered plinking further into the hall. On this recording I benefit from close microphones and the generous acoustic of the venue.

As I continue my drive toward campus, one of many commuters isolated in cars with our early morning preoccupations, I savor the relationships between the five instruments, the three inner voices functioning almost as a Greek chorus, seeming both to react to and to shape the more individually distinct actions of second cello and first violin. Toward the end of the first section I play longer and more pleading melodic phrases, my most individualistic foray so far. When I drop down a scale into the same register as the ongoing chords, the first cello takes the opportunity to emerge briefly as a descant at the top of the ensemble, a moment of lyrical independence that foreshadows a dramatic change of role in the middle section of this ABA-structured movement. To conclude the dialogue of rhythm and mood between second cello and first violin, there occurs a moment of agreement: just once we play the pizzicato rhythm together. Then, emerging from a trill and crescendo played by all five players, comes a violent transformation.

A young man bent against the wind and laden with a bulky backpack makes dogged progress against the wind, ears enveloped by large headphones as snowflakes melt in his long, dark hair. The light turns green as he reaches the sidewalk and I pull forward into the intersection, failing to notice a car that slides toward me from the left. Swerving at the last moment, I barely manage even the last two directives from my son's Driver Education course: Scan, Identify, Predict, Decide, Execute.

No amount of scanning would help to predict the sudden change of mood in the middle section of the Adagio. Keening high in the instrument's range, the first cello's melody withstands frantic fortissimo syncopations in the second violin and viola, insistent second beat jabs in the second cello, and vehement triplets exchanged back and forth. Above the first cello, I play the same melody one octave higher. An upper octave assignment can be treacherous: if one of my notes is just a fraction sharp or flat, the melody is soured (that suspicious cork again). But here I love my role in the drama, clinging to the first cello as we careen through breathless gestures before playing longer notes whose fragility is emphasized by the driving rhythms underneath.

After the extended control required to play the previous music, I find it cathartic to launch myself at this passage in which violence shatters serenity, the dark key of F minor displacing E major. But however brutal the rhythms or desperate the melodies, as a player I must maintain sufficient motor skills and awareness of my surroundings to remain together and in tune with the group. Traveling to the Takács studio this morning, I am made more aware of the derailing power of such wild music, the potential for anguish to subvert everyday routines. Perhaps driving under the influence of Schubert should be a ticketable offense.

Whereas the instability of this section depends in part on the way in which the musical lines fight with one another, once the outburst has exhausted itself all five players must come together to play fractured gestures that emerge from and return to silence. During rehearsals, reconciling the views of five strong-minded musicians can be a challenge: *The rests are too long—there's no tension in them—they're too short—we sound impatient—we should shape a phrase over the rests—that's too explicit a shape—I can't follow your sign—I don't want to be too obvious—it's so passive it sounds like we've died—that's how it should sound.*

It is no coincidence that Schubert demands unanimity at those pivotal transitions between contrasting music: the crescendo and trill that shatter the serene mood before plunging us into the middle section or the transition here that turns from unhinged anguish to a transformed final section. These are the crises where jolting changes of emotion, texture, and rhythm must be balanced by the greatest cooperation between the players. While pulses still race from the previous frenzy, the passage at the end of the middle section imposes a kind of physical and emotional discipline—the jarring individual manifestations of grief are merged, the distinctive characteristics of each player subsumed. Again, Schubert pulls the strings.

I turn off the main road into the campus and scan the icy bike path as a cyclist whizzes by, unperturbed by wind and snow. Unsettled by the music, I am relieved to park underneath a towering blue spruce tree. I can see only as far as the intersection, where the lights and road signs guide the journeys of those commuters heading toward the downtown. Lumps of snow fall periodically onto my windshield while I listen, already several minutes late to rehearsal.

The third section of the Adagio may return to the opening harmonies, but there is nothing repetitive or self-evident in the extraordinary transformation Schubert renders here. While the three inner voices return to their serene chords, the most startling invention is the rumbling of the second cello, ignoring the prior duties of a rhythm section, and instead producing a weird combination of fast upward forays and contrasting gestures that revolve insistently around one or two lower notes. With no rhythmic frame to resist or obey, the first violin takes its cue from the second cello, at first answering in contrary motion but then climbing upward—a more expansive, explicit version of its upward gestures in the opening section. Separated by the chords in between, the second cello and first violin are nonetheless entangled, an ascending run answered by a downward swoop, the two players sometimes coming together to play the same rhythms and dynamic gestures. This entwining of voices and sentiment is both sensual and ethereal.

Such arabesques cannot last. Now the second cello and first violin play the unyielding pizzicati together. Later the first violin tries to escape with more individual expressive gestures, its last attempt at independence realized in the form of two elaborate ornaments, expressive sighs and downward scales. Near the end of the Adagio the most emphatic pizzicato of all accentuates a moment of outburst that recalls the fury of the middle section—a final protest before a last E major chord that glows and then recedes into silence.

Schubert's extreme juxtaposition of serenity and tumult may expose the insignificant preoccupations of commuters as we grapple with the winter weather, traffic lights, and uncooperative signs, but my perspective this morning has been biased. Failing to notice the companionable carpoolers or the excited high schoolers piling out of a bus to attend a guided campus tour, I have been drawn to more isolated travelers and the obstructions they face: an irate postman, a self-absorbed student fighting against the wind, a construction worker and his unyielding STOP sign. But perhaps I only imagine their isolation in contrast to the intricate relationships I hear within the Adagio: relationships that are themselves a response to Schubert's own despair as "someone whose enthusiasm (whose creative inspiration at least) for all things beautiful threatens to fail," someone like the lonely traveler in the twentieth song of his song cycle *Winterreise*, "Der Wegweiser," who wonders what leads him to ignore the signposts that guide others, wandering restlessly, craving peace, until he comes across a sign that he cannot avoid: "I must travel a road / from which no one has returned."

After listening to this last section of the Adagio I experience a surprising sense of detachment from our recording. Removed from the physical, collaborative experience of playing with my colleagues it is harder to comprehend that I once contributed to this CD. I am aware instead of the transitory nature of chamber music ensembles and their performances. Feeling unmoored by my journey, I hoist my violin case onto my back, walking briskly toward the companionship of the Takács studio, eager to explore once again the duets, trios, individual flights of fancy and moments of consensus that Schubert has created; relationships that exist on a printed page, always awaiting new players and audiences.

6 Work Song

JEFF DOLVEN

When I was about seventeen, old enough to drive into Northampton on my own, I had an errand to run on a Saturday morning in the hardware store that used to be on Main Street. (Foster Farrar, it was called; they've moved to King Street since, but they're still in business.) I don't remember the errand now, and possibly I forgot it even then, because as soon as I walked in my attention was overtaken by what was playing on the store radio. It was a piece of music for flute—though I'm sure everything about that description already felt wrong. "For flute," wrong if only because there were so many of them, eleven I would learn, as much an ecology as an arrangement. "Piece of music," wrong because, coming in on the middle of it, it seemed as though it had always been playing, and would never come to an end. I found a quiet aisle among the tape measures and I stood still and listened. When it did end—I was taken so by surprise—the familiar voice of WFCR's morning host stepped clear of the labyrinth to say that it was called *Vermont Counterpoint* and that it had been written by a composer named Steve Reich in 1982, three years before. I went down the street to order the record. Possibly I went back to Foster Farrar for the sandpaper, or whatever it was I was supposed to get. Possibly I forgot all about it.

I have been listening to Reich's music ever since, catching up and then following along with a career that has lasted for more than fifty years. I used to have a stack of LPs, then CDs; now I dial it up on Spotify. I have heard *Drumming* (1971) and *Music for 18 Musicians* (1976) and *Different Trains* (1988) and others played in concert. But mostly, I listen while I work, while I read and write, as I am doing now. No music I know is so good for thinking with, and I've always wondered why—why his music serves so readily as the soundtrack (if "soundtrack" is the word) for the labor (if "labor" is the word) of the mind. Not everyone can listen to music while they work, and some music lovers and musicians find the practice dubious or disrespectful or even heretical. Among those who do it, who need it, I've talked to several over the years who share my dependence on Reich. His music is a kind of work song. Just now I've put him on again to see if I can work out why.

Work song: usually the phrase is used for songs sung to keep spirits up and bodies together in time. Many come from prisoners and slaves, whose work is bondage; songs like the ones Alan Lomax recorded in the 1940s, where the crack of the axe measures out the music and the task together. One of the Black prisoners he talked to at Parchman Farm in Mississippi explains that the work "go so better" when you sing with it, when you "keep [your] mind from being devoted on just one thing."[1] Writing is solitary, not collective; it is not physically taxing, it won't break you down, and it is almost never done under threat of violence. I risk the analogy only to credit that prisoner's hard-come-by insight about how the axe-falls and the rhythms of breathing at Parchman are brought into the music; the song is at the service of the work, pacing it and keeping it going, but at the same time, the work comes to be at the service of the song. The interdependence of labor and music makes the work go better than it could go alone, even if the work alone is brutal and unfree. That means work song is different from having a transistor radio playing on a construction site, where the music is a diversion but does not organize the activity or transform its meanings. It is that much more different from the soundtrack of retail, the buying-music for the customers that becomes the work-music of the employees, but work-music only by accidental association with their hours on the clock.

Listening now, back in my study, I am at a moment when the alto digs down to execute an intricate figure at the bottom of its register,

1 Alan Lomax, liner notes to *Prison Songs: Historical Recordings from Parchman Farm 1947–48*, vol. 1: *Murderous Home*, Rounder B000002UV, CD, 2009.

a figure that seems to store energy, like a flywheel, for an upward leap of a fifth—a big interval in a work so closely knit. Is it work, what I am doing, setting down these words? Work that has anything to do with the body's energy and exhaustion? How is it that the music could help? Someone watching me might be able to gather some sense of the fluctuations of my effort. I am writing longhand, though I'll type this paragraph up soon. There are moments when my brow furrows, my mouth tightens, when I lean forward and put my head in my hands. Thought is brought up short, its momentum breaks against a barrier, or dissipates into an unmarked clearing—some problem I cannot immediately solve, the right word, whatever it is, the next step. If there were a habit that would answer, the work would be easy. Hard is not having the habit, but having to probe, test, try, like a climber groping for the next hold. That's the feeling I have now. Hard for writing is when the pencil teeters between the sharp point and the eraser, or the hovering hand equivocates between the letters and the delete key. I am groping after the right metaphor. Perhaps a skipping record? The lost momentum is expressed in a kind of frustrated repetition.

That charge, that the music sounds like a skipping record, has been brought against Reich more than once, especially his first pieces. (An early audience member is said to have run up to the stage afterward and cried, "I confess!") *Vermont Counterpoint* falls somewhere in the early middle of his career, seventeen years after his experiments with phased tape loops (*It's Gonna Rain*, 1965) and his subsequent phased compositions for piano (*Piano Phase*, 1967) and violin (*Violin Phase*, 1967). Those earlier works are incremental canons, established by playing a short phrase in two-part unison, then gradually accelerating one of the parts to shift it out of phase with the other, displacing the unison by one note, then two, and so on. Skipping is precisely what these works do not do. Their change is perpetual. The emergent patterns of contrapuntal interference between the two lines define that change, which ends only when the accelerating player brings her part around to perfect unison again. *Vermont Counterpoint* builds on some of the same techniques. It begins with a syncopated seven-note phrase played by a single flute. Other parts enter one by one, doubling and displacing fragments of that first phrase so that it beats against itself, and gradually substituting notes for rests to create lines of increasing complexity and density.

You could perform the work with eleven players—three alto flutes, three flutes, three piccolos, and two soloists using all three—but it is usually heard live with a single soloist and tape. (Ransom Wilson commissioned it, and plays all eleven in the recording I first encountered.) In the density of the counterpoint, it is not always easy to discern the last part, the part that is listening to all the others. But that is the one that gives fullest articulation to the emerging melodies, melodies that extend the staccato phrases into more expansive, eloquent gestures. None lasts longer than about three measures before repeating and eventually subsiding into the shifting texture of canon around it. Still, each allows the continuous, repetitive process to become for a moment more expressive, and the work as a whole is always shifting its emphasis between engrossing background and the momentary salience of a new figure. Reich's earliest music insisted that the process be transparent throughout: "I am interested in perceptible processes. I want to be able to hear the process happening throughout the sounding music."[2] By *Vermont Counterpoint*, the sound of process is strong, but the demand for perfect, real-time intelligibility has been relaxed, and there is space for a melody that sounds, for a moment, as inspired as it does emergent.

Which is not to say that the dominant impression is of Romantic vaunting or sighing. Quite the contrary. Reich has said that the Western music that matters most to him was written between 700 and 1750. For Beethoven and Brahms and Mahler and even Mozart, he has little use. His music advances by the incremental development, the revolution and permutation, of discrete phrases, and the changes are always stepwise. If some steps are larger than others, still their dynamism does not depend on having a large sense of direction, on plotting the musicians' or the listeners' place in a long story. The musicologist Karol Berger writes about how composers before Mozart privilege the structures of figural variation, and how Mozart and his successors value the large-scale development

2 Steve Reich, *Writings on Music 1965–2000*, edited by Paul Hillier (Oxford: Oxford University Press, 2002), 34.

of narrative structure. (*Bach's Cycle, Mozart's Arrow* is the name of his book.)[3] Reich returns to the cycle by way of the phase, and his music, in its canonic *carmen perpetuum*, manages to be both unflaggingly energetic and infinitely patient. Significant cadences and modulations arise through the accumulation of small differences—purposiveness, you might say, without a purpose. Or thinking without a thought—unless the bright threads of melody are the momentarily thoughts, fleeting ideas; if so, they emerge and disappear, the next moment, into the texture of the thinking again.

So is this what writing is like? Or what writing should be like? Or at least, some protection for that fragile activity, some charm against what threatens it? Languor, to be sure, is a threat to the writer, and the unflagging pulse of Reich's counterpoint is an antidote—it has the drive of its regularity, and the fibrillating surprises of its syncopation. Distraction is another threat, the attention spinning off to pursue an unaccomplished errand or a curious bird. Reich's music is concentrated and self-continuous and insists that everything follow. Then there is the threat of too much focus, and again the music helps, for *Vermont Counterpoint* has a restless, lateral curiosity, a kind of concentration-as-distraction or distraction-as-concentration, always asking *what can be done with this? and with this? and what do we have now? and where might it go next?* It is music that keeps moving, as writing has to do, from note to note as from word to word. (The typically succinct notes, sharp attack, short decay, even on the flute, are almost spelled into phrases with white space between.) At the same time, its dynamism has a paradoxical power of reflection, of unhurried curiosity.

Which is to say that it is a mimesis of writing, or writing-thinking, a musical picture of it. What about doing the two together, listening and writing, as I am doing now? Thinking—now I'm really trying to think about it again, to feel it—somehow seems to happen in the front of my head, up above my eyes, and yet my whole body is caught up. In its pulse the music is autonomic, and it galvanizes the vagrant rhythms of breath and heartbeat into a kind of collaboration. I feel alert, how I imagine I would feel playing this music, entranced but

3 Karol Berger, *Bach's Cycle, Mozart's Arrow: An Essay on the Origins of Musical Modernity* (Berkeley: University of California Press, 2007).

not lulled, the intricate rhythm keeping the thinking moving and changing. The energy is immanent and it does not flag and does not, somehow, use me up or wear me out. Back at the beginning of his career, Reich wrote that "the pleasure I get from playing is not the pleasure of expressing myself, but of subjugating myself to the music and experiencing the ecstasy that comes from being a part of it."[4] Perhaps that is the feeling—of being part of one's own thinking, party to it, in some kind of immanent ecstasy; not dictated to, but borne along by the process of thought itself, in an even-tempered dialectic of continuity and surprise.

One might worry that such a music is the music of productivity, that what it is good for is keeping knowledge-workers working. And it is true that it is not passionate music, exactly, not the way, say, Mahler is—not music that imposes its emotional extremities on the listener, that aspires to disable us with vicarious grief or longing or exalt us with transports of pride and triumph. It is not music for writing love letters or eulogies. Its characteristic affect is the acute pleasure of experiencing your own sharpened faculties, almost as though the music were playing you, and so much more expertly than the jerky world does. Reich's work has never become the soundtrack for anyone's anesthetic capitalism; never so far as I know has it been used in an advertisement or as Muzak (*pace* the good NPR-listening carpenters of western Massachusetts). If he speaks of the pleasure of subjugation, it is just as much the pleasure of freedom—for again, though his music models thinking, it does not tell you what to think or where to go, doesn't steer your feelings through some story of its own, across the grain of your thought. If you have a plot to make, or an argument, what it affords you is a grid of attention across which the mind can move freely, in any direction, and yet still always forward.

Vermont Counterpoint has four sections; at the end of each, the counterpoint gradually falls away, and a residual melody is left to sound alone for a couple of bars before it begins to generate new canons. The third is slower than the others, but the level of detail is equally engrossing. I am there now. It is, again, not passionate mu-

4 Reich, *Writings*, 81–82.

sic. Nor is it music that defines the collectivity of its listeners by our common suffering. The work it is good for—the work it imagines, or incarnates—is not fallen work, not hard labor let alone slave labor. Still, I have cried listening to it, in concert, reliably, and now and again when a line ambushes me, even when I am writing. Not with a shudder of loss, as might pass through me in a late Beethoven quartet. The feeling is instead utopian—might our world be like this one, after all? The possibility arises of a ramifying, fractal, infinitely generous attention, at all scales at once, and a feeling—for this music is always for an ensemble, sharing rhythm as an intuition—that we are all in it together. Writing is a solitary business and it can stale. To wind it together with Reich's counterpoints is to remember the sheer beauty of the world, and to hold beauty, as Stendhal puts it, as a promise of happiness. A work song for good work freely undertaken, carried along and carried through. It is good luck to be able to do it. My period, as it happens, falls not on the last note, but somewhere in the middle.

7 Arvo Pärt's *Tabula Rasa*

CORINNA DA FONSECA-WOLLHEIM

I first heard Arvo Pärt as a teenager during the summer after the fall of the Berlin Wall. I was a participant at an international youth music festival in Scotland where one of the visiting groups was a chamber ensemble from Estonia. In the festival orchestra I shared a desk in the second violin section with one of the players, who struck me as aloof and scarily accomplished. At their concert the Estonians performed Britten's *Simple Symphony* alongside a work called *Cantus* written to memorialize Britten's death. The printed program identified the composer of that work as Arvo Pärt, Estonian, and living. I remember noting the last name with interest, surprised by the appearance of an umlaut in an East Bloc language.

Most unexpected was the impact of the *Cantus* itself, a dirge of forbidding beauty with pealing bells and thick-flowing strings that seeped down a minor scale with the cumulative mass and languorous ferocity of lava. Sitting in the audience with fellow students, I was struck by the music's austere grandeur. Pärt's style bore no comparison to that of any other contemporary composer I had encountered. With its monochrome wash of a single tonality, the piece was transparently accessible, yet filled with taut dissonances, many sustained for uncomfortable stretches of time. The emotional tenor of the piece was hard to pin down, somehow both tender and unyielding in its grief. I would have liked to have asked one of the musicians about it after the concert, but though my childhood in Belgium had left me with a good grip on four languages, they offered no common ground with Estonian and Russian. The linguistic barrier added to the mystery of Pärt's work. Even so, that performance of *Cantus* represented a rent in the Iron Curtain, and what I had glimpsed through it seemed remote yet familiar.

When I heard *Cantus* again the following year, I felt the thrill mixed with relief you experience when you bump into someone you've given up for lost after an unexpectedly significant chance encounter. This time I had someone to discuss it with. I had entered a somewhat lopsided friendship with a conductor I had met in a youth orchestra. I was eighteen and about to embark on a music degree in England, keen to fill the gaps in my knowledge and hungry for new experiences. He was some ten years older and in a relationship, though that didn't stop a crackle of sexual tension from mingling with the cigarette smoke during the long evenings we spent talking and listening to music in his living room. One topic that was dear to him was the concept of space in music, a quality he had long loved in symphonies of Bruckner and Mahler, and that had now drawn him to the works of Pärt. "I like music where I feel I can breathe," he said. He had a CD that contained *Cantus* as well as a work for two solo violins, prepared piano, and string orchestra called *Tabula Rasa*.

In this piece the sense of space really was palpable, both in its silences—the horizontal space between sounds—and in the vertical chasm created by very high notes soaring above deep basses. The sporadic interventions of the prepared piano added a sound unlike any I'd heard before, a dull metallic gurgle that appeared to rise from deep under water. The music seemed to require a whole new way of listening, a simultaneous abandonment of thought and clarity of focus that, perhaps for the first time, promised to still the chatter of my self-conscious teenage mind. It wasn't long before I bought a copy of the recording and *Tabula Rasa* became an emotional anchor in my choppy transition to adulthood.

Tabula rasa means "clean slate." But although Pärt's music did possess a cool stillness that felt utterly new, it also connected to a much older musical touchstone of mine. Perhaps it's not untypical that what felt like a discovery all of my own was in fact closely entwined with my musical DNA. Up until then much of my taste in classical music was inherited. I grew up in a German family living in Brussels. My parents, who worked in the institutions of the European Union, were both from Hamburg and had brought with them a deep attachment to music that was solidly rooted in Bach. Their record collection contained large chunks of Mozart and Beethoven as well as the lieder by Schubert and Schumann, but the lion's share was given over to Bach, whose music also spilled over into ritual. On Sundays we sang his hymns in the German-speaking Lutheran congregation of Brussels; on Christmas Eve the jubilant opening of his Christmas Oratorio rang in the exchange of presents.

I began violin lessons around my seventh birthday. I was no prodigy, so it was only in my preteens, when I tackled Bach's Violin Concerto in A Minor, that my instrumental studies merged with the family musical canon. My parents had a recording of the concerto, and for the first time I snuck an album from their collection up to my bedroom to play in private. That was the moment Bach became part of my musical medicine cabinet.

The record also included the violin concerto in E and the one for two violins in D minor. All three contain slow movements that hover between profound melancholy and sweet hopefulness, and it was those "downers" tucked in between the fast-movement "uppers" that I started to crave the most. I drew special comfort from the Largo of the double violin concerto in which the solo voices engage in a wistful dance that unspools easily, equally. Both players take turns with one heavyhearted descending line and one that loops above and around it in graceful arabesques. Over time I came to play the Bach Double with a variety of partners, including cousins, friends, and potential romantic partners, and with each reading its slow movement took on new hues, from consolation and reconciliation to freedom.

Much of the aching loveliness of that Largo comes from the suspensions created when one violin sustains a consonant note while the other moves on, changing the underlying harmony and creating temporary dissonance until the first voice follows suit and restores consonance. Suspensions are common in Baroque music. I grew to love them through the chamber music I sight-read with friends in my youth, from simple Telemann duets to trio sonatas by Handel and Bach's *Musical Offering*. One reason I responded so strongly to the device as an adolescent is that suspensions mirrored familiar psychological and interpersonal dynamics. In the clinging to and releasing of a temporarily "wrong" note, they echoed the feeling of holding on to something you knew you couldn't reasonably keep, the dragging of feet on the road to purported maturity. And there was something wonderfully apt in the fact that the equal distribution of roles, with each musical voice acting alternately as pull and as dead weight, created both perfect balance and constant friction. The lines rubbed together and separated in a way that was erotically charged yet unhurried, even aimless, in much the same way I recall meandering evenings of mutual confessions and booze with boys. Anthropomorphized, the two violins in Bach's Largo seem not so much lovers as friends with benefits.

If I go to these lengths talking about Bach, it's because Pärt's *Tabula Rasa* is a double violin concerto—and its slow movement teems with suspensions. Pärt wrote it in 1976 as he emerged from an eight-year period of self-imposed silence. He had studied music in Tallinn during the Khrushchev era and had experimented with serialism in his early compositions, a style rejected by Soviet orthodoxy as decadent. But it was his choral work *Credo*, written in 1968, that triggered political repercussions for its overtly liturgical nature.

For eight years, Pärt published nothing and composed little, applying himself instead to the study of early music. During this time he also converted from the Lutheran to the Russian Orthodox faith. When he broke his silence it was with a new musical style he came to call "tintinnabuli," for the Latin word for small bells. His music now had a distinctive meditative quality, with spare textures, hypnotic repetitions of simple patterns, and a radiant, unwavering single key. That recognizable key set these pieces aside from the atonal scores of Pärt's modernist contemporaries and lured in audiences who were otherwise alienated by new music. And yet Pärt's tonality didn't behave like traditional tonality—there was none of the eventfulness, the narrative tension that underpins much of Western music. The familiar outlines of, say, an A-minor scale make it easy to enter a composition, but once there, the mind is bidden to contemplate a single, still entity in a way that can reflect the attention back onto the listener. Whether that kind of void feels exhilarating or scary can depend on the day.

Before long the subject matter of virtually all Pärt's compositions became overtly Christian, a development helped by the fact that he slipped out of reach of the Soviet censors and moved to the West.

There, Pärt quickly became a new-music sensation, topping charts and attracting followers in the most unexpected quarters, all the while maintaining his monkish humility. Even his purely instrumental works were infused with Christianity. That's because central to his new style was the triad, representing the Holy Trinity. Tintinnabuli composition consists of two lines: a melody voice, which moves in small steps along a horizontal axis, and a tintinnabuli voice, which toggles between the component notes of a vertically stacked triad. The algorithm that gives shape to a piece is usually transparent and stunningly simple: in *Cantus* the string instruments all play the same downward scale but at different speeds; in *Tabula Rasa* melodies are built up patiently by adding a single note to a cell each time it is repeated, first on the way up, then on the descent.

For all its purported break with the past, Pärt's *Tabula Rasa* and its companion pieces declare their allegiance to an unbroken musical history that always passes through Bach. One of Pärt's serial compositions from the 1960s had used the notes spelling out B-A-C-H (in German nomenclature, the notes B-flat, A, C, B-natural); his *Credo* quoted from Bach's limpid Prelude No. 1 in C. Bach references also abound in a piece sparkling with humor that imagined the baroque master as a beekeeper. *Tabula Rasa* itself was written in response to a commission that sought an overt link to Baroque music. The violinist Gidon Kremer had already requested a concerto grosso from the Soviet composer Alfred Schnittke, who chose the unorthodox instrumentation of two solo violins, prepared piano, and chamber orchestra. *Tabula Rasa* was intended as a companion to that work.

Tabula Rasa consists of two parts, one, brilliant and animated, called "Ludus" ("game"), and an extensive slow one called "Silentium." "Ludus" opens with a fortissimo double A played by the solo violins at the upper and lower edges of their register that tears through the silence and disappears into it, leaving a silent void. After a long pause, the orchestra enters with a pattern built from the three notes of the A-minor triad and slow A-minor scales. The solo voices dance high above in filigree arpeggios and gleaming, spidery lines. Gradually their parts are consumed by the orchestral texture, which grows thicker, louder, and more jagged, culminating in an angry cadence. The movement ends with the same fortissimo chord that opened it, now played tutti and held with sustained ferocity.

An upward-bubbling arpeggio from the piano introduces the second movement, now in D minor, which again rests on a single pattern, imitated across sections of the orchestra, of a rising and falling motif over a languidly drawn-out descending scale. Fragile and delicate, the soloists' parts soar high above the orchestra and piano. Their motion proceeds so slowly that their descent down the scale is almost imperceptible. When they reach the bottom of their register and hand the motif down to the lower strings in the orchestra, the effect is surprising and inevitable.

The movement titled "Silentium" lasts over a quarter of an hour —an eternity in pop music and even in the context of a classical concerto. For Gidon Kremer the premiere of the work held unexpected challenges, despite its apparent simplicity on the page. "For seventeen minutes one hardly dared to breathe, because there was the danger it would affect the movement of the bow," he said in an interview. In a Bach concerto the slow movement is always followed by an exuberant fast one. Here, the calm is final, and lasting. The critic Alex Ross wrote of terminally ill AIDS patients requesting *Tabula Rasa* in the final stages of their battle with the disease. They called it "angel music."

I discovered *Tabula Rasa* at a moment in my life when I was trying to figure out who I wanted to be. As in the Largo of Bach's Concerto for Two Violins, I found in it solace and a model of an ideal relationship that was equal and free. But where Bach came with the baggage of family and tradition, Pärt seemed—at least for a while—all mine. Perhaps the secret of the work's appeal is that the slate feels blank yet viscerally familiar. It also contains an invitation to inscribe yourself. In the last bars of "Silentium" the basses complete their descent so quietly that you almost don't notice that they end on the penultimate note of the scale.

It's the listener who is left to supply the final note and take responsibility for the work's resolution.

8 On Chopin's Ballade No. 2, Op. 38

JAMIE BARTON

My world changed when I heard Chopin for the first time. It was late at night, and I had a shoddy pair of earphones on to keep my little brother from complaining to our parents about my late-night listening session. The opening strains of Ballade No. 2 in F began to play, and it felt like the perfect music to go to sleep to: serene, calm, beautiful. I remember the volume seeming a little low, so I cranked it up a notch. There was nothing but the absolute darkness of a country night in my eyes, and this hushed musical tranquility of Chopin in my ears. . . .

//

I grew up in the foothills of the Appalachian Mountains in a sleepy little valley known to the locals as "The Pocket." Johns Mountain and Horn Mountain come together on the northern end of our valley to create a pocket; hence, the name. Many generations of my family have lived in that valley. My great-grandfather, Lloyd Barton, purchased a one-room house in The Pocket back in the 1930s. After adding on a handful of rooms to accommodate his wife and children, he moved his family into that little house. Fifty years later, I was born, and spent the first six years of my life living in that very same home.

When I was six, my parents decided they wanted to build on the portion of land that my grandparents had set aside for my dad. And so, we moved from my great-grandfather's house into a single-wide trailer, directly across the street. My parents never did build that house of their dreams, so the temporary trailer on our family land became the backdrop for the formative years of my life.

To this day, my family's land is just about as "off the map" as you can get. Until 2018, there wasn't even running water provided by the county—residents of The Pocket had to dig and maintain their own wells. However, what we did have in abundance was nature. Beautiful, serene, and often lonely, nature surrounded us. I loved sitting in my bay window and looking over the field, imagining that characters from my books would emerge from the forest to play with me and keep me company.

While it might sound isolated, I also had an incredibly close-knit family. As it happens, music was a way my family often connected. Cousins, aunts, and uncles would bring their bluegrass instruments to big family gatherings, and we would all make music together. My great aunt Emogene and great uncle Carl would host "pickin and grinnin's," inviting the entire valley to show up at their place with their string instruments and a potluck dish and spend the evening jamming with their neighbors. Even within our own household, music was something almost sacred. I remember sitting as a child and listening to albums with my family—my little brother and I weren't allowed to run around the trailer when an album was playing, lest it skip. As a result, music was something I learned to pay attention to. I heard the storytelling from every angle: words, music, rhythm. Strains of classic rock and bluegrass music filled my ears and hooked me into musical storytelling from a very early age. It's these genres of music I return to even now when I'm homesick and need to feel connected to the earth.

And then came Nirvana.

In 1991, my little brother brought my attention to this new musical experience. Nirvana changed the available soundscape as we knew it. I had literally never heard anything like "Smells Like Teen Spirit." Nirvana, with its jagged, rough, explosive melodies and wailing front man, opened my ears to a world of music I barely knew existed. This is not a story of Nirvana or how that band changed my musical life (or, as one might argue, the direction of my life as a whole), but the discovery of Nirvana inspired curiosity for the world outside of my serene little bubble in a way that nothing else had. I was on the edge of adolescence, and my mind was spinning with this newfound knowledge. Where had this music come from? What else was out there? Why did I connect so immediately with something I was just beginning to discover?

My "tween" brain was hooked. I put aside my parents' bluegrass and classic rock collections, and started to try to figure out what else was out there. This was not easy for a kid who didn't have a driver's license, who lived in an area with no cable television, and who was certainly coming of age before the internet was readily available. Slowly but surely, I found my way, carved my own path. Some college-aged counselors with whom I worked at a local Boy Scout camp introduced me to classic rock bands that my parents had never really listened to, and I fell in love: Pink Floyd, Led Zeppelin, and Simon & Garfunkel became the bridge between something familiar and something very new to me.

Acquiring recordings of this new music was no small feat. I had no allowance, so purchasing recordings was just out of the question. I did, however, have a little boombox that sat at the head of my bed. I began to spend most of my evenings alone in my room, finishing up homework while listening to the radio. I had some blank cassette tapes, and I would keep one in the boombox at all times so that if I liked what was playing on the radio, I could hit record and keep it for myself. Frequently, that was alternative rock. But late at night, after the sun set over Johns Mountain and the only sound in the valley was that of the occasional coyote or owl, I would listen to the NPR station out of Chattanooga, Tennessee.

The nighttime radio host of WUTC, 88.1 FM radio, had an affinity for Romantic-era composers. While the rest of my household slept, my ears were filled night after night with the sounds of Tchaikovsky and Mahler. I fell in love with composers of other eras: J. S. Bach with his mathematical and mind-blowing fugues, Mozart with his *Requiem* (before I knew anything about the piece, I would swear I could hear the weeping in the "Lacrimosa" movement). Composers like Erik Satie brought a smile to my face with his charming musical sarcasm, and I was endlessly intrigued by Maurice Ravel's *Gaspard de la nuit*. These were incredibly evocative stories that I could hear unfold wordlessly. While Nirvana amplified emotions that already existed within me, classical music took me on journeys into parts of my imagination that I hadn't even known existed. However, no journey was quite as beautiful or entrancing to me as the music of Frédéric Chopin.

//

So there I was on that unforgettable night, listening to Chopin for the first time, being lulled toward sleep by the placid opening of Chopin's Ballade No. 2 in F.

And then the *presto con fuoco* hit.

My eyes shot open with the sound of a screaming piano flooding those inadequate earphones. The change in mood jolted me out of any hope of sleep I might have had. My heart pounded as I absorbed the jarring shift in musical storytelling. The right hand of the pianist sounded like a wild animal desperately trying to escape entrapment, and I listened as the left hand seemed to work to soothe the upper hand's madness with repeated upward scales. When the madness passed and the *tempo primo* returned, my heart was still racing. I listened to the rest of the piece with every fiber of my being, as if it were the last sound I would ever hear.

Years later in a musicology course in college, I would learn that Chopin had dedicated this ballade to Robert Schumann, whose struggle with clinical depression was well known. The manic shifts between the moods of the *andantino* and the *presto con fuoco* sections suddenly took on a new meaning for me.

From that night on, I was absolutely hooked on Chopin's music. I heard his *Fantaisie-Impromptu* and craved more. The polonaises and waltzes that my late-night NPR radio DJ dropped into my soundscape made me want to dance to the music, and the "Raindrop" Prelude was balm to my emo teenager soul.

I began to ask my family for classical music recordings, specifically those of Chopin. And so, for my birthday and Christmas, that's precisely what I received. (I think my extended family was delighted to have some solid direction on what to buy their teenage family member, albeit likely very confused . . . when did Jamie start listening to classical music??) Someone gifted me a box set of "Classical Music's Greatest Composers!," and the Mozart CD introduced me to the soaring vocals of the Queen of the Night. Another family member bought me a compilation CD of Italian arias; I still have fond memories of Anna Moffo singing "Una voce poco fa" from *Il Barbiere di Siviglia* by Gioachino Rossini, and wondering how on earth someone could sing that quickly. (I still wonder that when listening to great coloratura singers!) But the gem that came my way in the form of a compilation compact disc—a disc that still ranks among my absolute favorite CDs—was an album entitled *Chopin and Champagne*.

Chopin and Champagne was a treasure trove of some of the most beautiful recordings of Chopin's music. With the exception of one track (Berceuse in D-flat, Op. 57, expertly played by Nikita Magaloff), the entire album is performed by the late and great Claudio Arrau. The opening and closing tracks of this disc (the *Larghetto* of Piano Concerto No. 2 in F Minor, and the *Romanze: Larghetto* of Piano Concerto No. 1 in E Minor, respectively) are accompanied by the London Philharmonic Orchestra. On this side of my long love for classical music, I can confidently say that while the title of this album may seem ridiculous, this is not a shabby cast of players at all.

I loved this recording immediately. Claudio Arrau seemed to understand instinctively the shape of Chopin's music. The peaks and valleys of those soaring phrases were so masterfully played that his recordings opened my ears and mind to beauty I had never dared imagine. However, what caught me about this recording, and what has me returning to this recording even now, is that I could hear how absolutely swept up Claudio Arrau was in playing the music of Chopin. Studio recordings are often so pristine, each note perfectly in place without a hint of extraneous noise. But what I loved about this particular recording was that I could hear Maestro Arrau breathing with the music. I could hear his sharp intakes of breath at various points and feel when he was holding his breath, only to be rewarded with gentle exhalations when the music released him to breathe again. At age fourteen, in the isolation of the north Georgia mountains, I felt deeply connected to someone I had never met—someone who had died only a handful of years earlier—because we both understood the utter breathlessness the beauty of Chopin's music could inspire.

I fell so in love with his recordings of Chopin's music that I listened to this CD until the disc would no longer play. (Thank goodness for the digital age of music—it brought this recording back into my life!) As much as I love the recordings of other great Chopin interpreters such as Evgeny Kissin and Krystian Zimerman, they have never been able to hold a candle to Claudio Arrau for me.

Why is that, you ask?

I think the answer comes down to what binds many of us to music: a visceral link into storytelling, where your experience is limited only by your imagination. There is magic in finding our favorite musical interpreters to guide us through the peaks and valleys of our musical journeys, and a sort of loyalty that enables those musicians to live on in our ears long after they have passed away. Music is a place where we can feel a personal connection to something truly extraordinary, beautiful, and available to us all, no matter the constraints of time, location, class, or age. This is a gift freely given for all to enjoy.

The other masters of Chopin's music have produced some of the most beautiful recordings on earth. However, only one recording reached across time and space to make a shy girl from the middle of virtually nowhere—with no connection to classical music whatsoever other than a cheap pair of earphones, a boom box, and an NPR station blessedly within range—feel seen and understood. It was through a comically named compilation CD of the works of Chopin that I fell in love with the art of wordless, musical storytelling, and it was the soft noise of Arrau's enraptured breathing that breathed such life into my new love that I was forever changed.

What a gift, indeed.

Pleyel 9

SUSAN STEWART

The reader in the garden, the reclining
granite nude.

A bevy of wrens, invisible,
but audible,

a silent cardinal's splash of red . . .

"Wait, wait a minute," the pupil mutters and the
teacher tucks the metronome back behind its
lid, and closes the brass latch,

and softly claps, then takes up the pencil-stub to
draw a stop.
The fig leaves bristle through their five-

finger exercises, the figs slowly
ripen, ripening.
The pupil hears the pages turn behind him in
the garden.

The goldfish circles and circles the glass.

How far from the sea, those small
elations of the garden . . .
The sky is as tame as a pane of glass.

“Nothing lasts, nothing lasts,” say the
white keys and the black,
“Arch your fingers, use your thumbs,” says

the weary teacher. Counting, counting, then
climbing, through time. A face, a line,
a memory of Autumn in the distance,

the wind wrapping, rapping, a cascade
of littered twigs. Beneath the bristling leaves, the
striped fruit ripening.

The goldfish circles and circles the glass.

Two worlds, within and without the long windows. A
melody, a harmony, a lack,
a patch of green. And then there are four—

the book, the slow unwinding,
the sky as calm as, say, a pane of glass. And
then there are six—the day-dreaming

boy and the teacher, who has glimpsed
a red fleck through the leaves. A small start in a
small sound, a break in noise or silence,

that amplifies to loud, louder, loudest. A
flicked paint brush, a meandering baton.
“Wait, wait, a minute,”

he says to no one waiting. Where is the time,
the time the music occupies? And where
is the time that it still evades, assuages?

The reader turns a page that ends and doesn’t, mid-
sentence. The goldfish circles
and circles the glass. Suspended, the boy, like

every good boy, does fine.

Far beyond the garden and the town, the
sea rages. And at
its edge, in solitude, a

cow eats grass.

10 Jessye Norman Sings "Die Nachtigall" by Alban Berg

ALICIA HALL MORAN AND JASON MORAN

The Nightingale	*Die Nachtigall*, by Theodor Storm
It is because the nightingale	Das macht, es hat die Nachtigall
Has sung throughout the night,	Die ganze Nacht gesungen;
That from the sweet sound	Da sind von ihrem süssen Schall,
Of her echoing song	Da sind in Hall und Widerhall
The roses have sprung up.	Die Rosen aufgesprungen.
She was once a wild creature,	Sie war doch sonst ein wildes Blut,
Now she wanders deep in thought;	Nun geht sie tief in Sinnen;
In her hand a summer hat,	Trägt in der Hand den Sommerhut
Bearing in silence the sun's heat,	Und duldet still der Sonne Glut
Not knowing what to do.	Und weiß nicht, was beginnen.
It is because the nightingale	Das macht, es hat die Nachtigall
Has sung throughout the night,	Die ganze Nacht gesungen;
That from the sweet sound	Da sind von ihrem süssen Schall,
Of her echoing song	Da sind in Hall und Widerhall
The roses have sprung up.	Die Rosen aufgesprungen.

JASON: When Alicia and I were students at Manhattan School of Music we often held hands while sitting in concerts.

> It is because the nightingale
> Has sung throughout the night . . .

The concerts ranged from oratorio (I specifically recall one that featured Reverend Jesse Jackson as narrator) to student jazz and voice recitals, to Milton Babbitt evenings. During our courting period lots of aesthetic bars were established. We would rattle off our favorite composers.... I'd often say "Oh, you know what you have to hear?!" and off we'd go proving to each other how much we had listened to. My must-hear list revolved mostly around golden era hip-hop because hip-hop in New York during the '90s was quaking the world.

> ... from the sweet sound
> Of her echoing song
> The roses have sprung up.

Everything bursting and open, emerging straight from the five boroughs into an international marketplace. But ironically it was in those years that my ear shifted further toward classical music because dating Alicia—and accompanying her on piano—meant learning the classic vocal literature. "From spirituals to Schumann" was an often-trod road. Every once in a while the road led to Ellington, which always made me happy.

ALICIA: Composers write songs. If you want to get closer to a composer, you check out their songs, especially their earliest songs. If they are good composers, then all their first longing is there. Maybe they haven't mastered yet what to hide or hold back, or how to pace themselves. You can mine that.

JASON: Before we met, Alicia studied composition while attending Barnard College, and one of her professors shared his love of Alban Berg with the class. The day that Alicia said, "Oh, you know what you *must* hear ...," it was Alban Berg's Violin Concerto. I listened. The way the harmony slid around, I couldn't anticipate the changes, the way they exuded total emotion. Berg registered immediately as Duke Ellington's cousin across the water. And that is how I listened from then on. Listening for my language.

ALICIA: Jason, that's the echo! Someone or something against which to sound out, yes, but it's when that sound comes back that we recognize our own voice in there. And because it sounds familiar we embrace it readily. We echo each other, or we are looking for . . . sonar . . . sending waves out, feeling for what comes back. I measure my life against yours in a way that shows me where I am. I learn a lot from your life, next to mine. I think it shows us better who we are. I think I give you good advice because I am right next to you and your choices affect mine.

JASON: Alicia shared this music with me, testing me, or even my love, as if to ask, "Can you even handle this?"

She was once a wild creature,

And I could.

ALICIA: My choral director in high school, Mr. Jesse Chapman, he'd always say that the music was already in the air, that we only needed to reach out and grab it. He would begin with a hum and we would "find" the frequency of our music with our voices. "Trust that the music is already there. Don't reach. Just join it."

Our voices joined the hum in the air. Our minds joined in the air. We experienced euphony. Harmony flows outward from this place.

//

Jessye Norman sang as one body, always in harmony with herself. It's a qualitative statement for sure, but I don't think I've ever read an argument to the contrary. Critics love to write about a singer who has what they call great control, but with Jessye, I don't even think about the idea of control. Her virtuosity sails past that concern at too rapid a pace. It's like we are on the ride with her. There's too much to listen to, and so much stimulus, too many parts of the musicianship firing at once.

Sie war doch sonst ein wildes Blut,
Nun geht sie tief in Sinnen;
Trägt in der Hand den Sommerhut

Und duldet still der Sonne Glut
Und weiß nicht, was beginnen.

These five lines deliver us to the B section and a change of focus. Time decelerates in this syrupy spot while the poet turns our attention from the nightingale's song to the inner world of the roses, and the one whose passion runs so deep, the poet marks her "wildes Blut" (wild blood).

JASON: We'd just been in the tonic key D major for "die Rosen aufgesprungen," and now this is a dramatic shift into F-sharp minor . . .

ALICIA: . . . the beautiful shift here sweeps you up into a new space, a transition into reverie, a sort of passionate trance. The humidity here is palpable. Berg is flirting with us. Berg is doing to our harmonic bodies what the roses were made to feel at the song of the Nightingale.

She was once a wild creature,
Now she wanders deep in thought;
In her hand a summer hat,
Bearing in silence the sun's heat,
Not knowing what to do.

And here we are, with our roses sprung. Die Nachtigall, the nightingale, issued a sweet call resulting in a blatant act of musical procreation. Now in the B section we take the temperature of the scene, we analyze the crux of the poem. Everything goes deeper here, warmer, in sultry voice. I'd argue that heat is beyond beauty. Heat is another way of listening. Heat in singing relates to the blood, its rhythmic pulse and flow, the work of the heart, the source of heat in the body and even the temperature of the air in our lungs before it is sung out and reaches the ears of the listener. Is it still *alive*? How does this warmth reach us, acoustically? A great singer always makes me feel that their lips are very close to my ear. Almost that sound is traveling in reverse—from my ear to their throat.

This warm, well-rounded, flexible legato singing with notes sustained in tune with overtones emanating from the head requires the absolute greatest opposite grounding and stability below, in the solar plexus and the diaphragm, the "legs" of the voice. The sensation of balance in the body is not heroically muscular, however. It is a practiced system of balance and poise, the slightest tension and an equal resistance to that tension. But in the breath, somehow.

Jessye's furnace-like capacity to generate one deep, warm phrase after another—that impresses me. It is the color of her voice and the quality of her *speaking through* her singing voice that attract me to the recording. With a German dictionary I can understand the German words. But Jessye Norman understood the German language.

//

We enter a singing lesson. In English, "Nightingale" is pronounced so brightly. Even the [a] in "night" is bright. We'll use the front of the facial resonance, the gums supporting the first teeth, the tip of the tongue, and just a stroke of the hard palate to pronounce the [g] to the point of registering a slight click closer to [k] than [g]. Make these sounds.

Aspiring opera singers are instructed diligently in how to barely pressurize the initial [n] so that the tip of the tongue only taps the very front of the hard palate, a place approximately where the teeth end and the gums begin. Exhaling air simultaneously buzzing behind that [n] must not cause the throat to close behind it, must not ask the back of the tongue to grab from deeper in the throat; the feeling is akin to holding a door open for yourself and then keeping it open for the person behind you. We sustain without collapse.

We have to get this vowel up in the air. When it takes flight, that vowel becomes the canvas onto which a poem is then painted in expressive tones. Color. Syntax. "Die Nachtigall" as a poem, as a composition, and especially as sung by Jessye Norman, is a master class in all of these things.

Continuing on. In English, the *nightingale*'s first "ah" sound emerges naturally once the tongue is released from the [n], and the jaw drops slightly to allow for a larger cavern inside the mouth, but gently, lest we disturb the stream of air too much. Or, in some cases, the space of the pharynx above and beyond the tongue balloons out to allow more space, in conjunction with or instead of lowering the jaw. Ms. Norman's approach seemed to embrace a consistent unhinging of the jaw paired with great use of the pharyngeal cavern, as well as a masterly employment of the lips and vestibule, the interior portion of the lower lip, and the gingivae, the gums covering the upper and lower teeth.

Once [n] is tapped and just as soon as [a] is placed, this word *nightingale* asks our mouths to allow a diphthong: the *seamless* glide from one vowel into another vowel without a consonant interrupting the flow of air. Aaaaa to a softer variation of eeee is required to sing the word "night." Try it, and feel that word *night*, drawn out slowly, in your mouth. If you love that, then you have a singer inside.

In German, the capacity for the sound [a] or "ahhh" darkens considerably. You move from the bright [a] in "night" to the dark [a] we hear in "father." And for German we must enter the symbol [x], the deep guttural "cht" that lies low in the throat designed by the back of the tongue, similar to what is found in Hebrew and Arabic. *Night* goes to *Nacht*, adding a mimetic psychoacoustic layer.

We attach our understanding to the language of our thoughts. A great singer is thinking in the language of her song. She is communicating with a conductor in the language of the composer. Even the beginning student, once obsessed, will respond to her teacher, "Ja" instead of "Yes," if given the chance. Or a Parisian tourist, quick to enjoy a quick "Oui," if he can slip it into dialogue with a local. I think so much of my father, too, a licensed captain and recreational sailor, who will speak to me immediately in boating jargon, whether I understand or not, the moment I step onto his boat. Such is a practitioner absorbed in the sea of her chosen language.

//

ALICIA: Jason, do you feel any symmetry with Jessye Norman, her being raised in the American South and then ending up interpreting music from around the world?

JASON: I don't know. We take our own histories into account. Sometimes it is not about leaving home. As an artist it can be more about going where we have to go to have the conversations we need to have for our Art.

ALICIA: Leaving home, leaving the familiar, leaving the people who first educated us, leaving one support system. Finding an audience but also finding new stages. For me, Jessye Norman is both the rose and the bird that calls herself up and out into the world.

The nightingale's world grows around us while we listen. Stressed syllables of important words are pulled long for emphasis, and for the sheer physical sensation of it, and tones are interpolated upward to signal the uncontainable, unrestrained, inner bubbling of Life itself. Berg's setting of Theodor Storm's poem pulsates around the text.

Da sind von ihrem süssen Schall

... we rise in pitch, then we lengthen *süssen* (sweet) to allow space for the depth of our emotional commitment to the word. Words requiring great amounts of breath mean to mimic greater amounts of emotional attachment. Length and effort go together: you cannot sustain something for a long time in music and not really mean it. Length *is* meaning. Because more than anything else, music is time. Music slows time so effectively. It can just take forever to sing a sentence. And in the body, it feels like forever. And therein is the bulk of the pleasure. Invisible to an audience, yet audible. In Jessye Norman, the pleasure is visible and audible. Her gift to us.

Da sind in Hall und Widerhall   From the reverberation and echo

When Jessye Norman sings these words she in effect breaks the curse of the Greek muse Echo, who was reduced to nothing but her voice after Narcissus would only love himself. Jessye Norman, our Nightingale, finds her love matched in Nature. The song is a triumph of love—the nocturnal kind—but also a triumph of the Singer.

The sequence rises up another half step in pitch, and "Widerhall" rises in pitch and stretches itself like a cat in the window. All echo is rhythm marking the sonic space between two objects set at a distance. In the oceanic voice of Jessye Norman, I hear a space where sound and the Earth are combining. The timbral darkness of her tones, the entirety of her skull reverberant with tone and quality. There are so many resonant chambers in the head: the dome of the skull, the dome of the mouth (hard palate), all the tunneling sinus ways and even all the smaller softer spaces we call joints, where a different kind of tissue softens the spaces where bone meets bone. There are inches of space in the lower jawbone allowing the tongue to lie down in its bed, and all the ways we swallow and inhale are protected by their own canals. The head is a miraculous feat of plumbing and, like any room filled with pipes and ducts, is a place for wild acoustic opportunity. And it is here, too, where the spine passes up from the back, along the throat, and straight into the head, ending someplace up between the ears or eyes, where it finally connects to mission control: the brain. The way Jessye's voice finds new planes in the space of the head—that most of us do not even know we have—is its own miracle. It allowed her to speak the language of being human, something anatomical that goes far, far beyond language, experience, and dialect. It is old and relevant as bones.

I do not know what Jessye Norman imagined when she opened her mouth to sing. How did she herself conceive of her Universe of mouth? The ocean of tongue and terrain of lip and atmosphere of belly and bellows, delicate and dancing hands, diaphragm and chest, all of which she manifested in one body—and maneuvered?

I listen to her and it is as if the orchestra is playing from inside the cavern of her head. Many singers of her caliber display exquisite artistry, but they do not all possess the physical capability to do this, to play all the colors of the orchestra from one body.

So when Ms. Norman sings these lines, we can believe that something vibrates in musical procreation, from which Nature can be born.

Die Rosen aufgesprungen.	The roses have sprung up.

Jessye's vocal arc finds ecstatic frequency, and with her "aufgesprungen" the voice pours out along the page, along the landscape—expanding time—as the note rises before resolving.

She was once a wild creature,
Now she wanders deep in thought;
In her hand a summer hat,
Bearing in silence the sun's heat,

> I am the warmth of my mother as she speaks the letters of the word *Mississippi* in rhythm, her special way of making spelling lessons more fun. They are all in my DNA: their beautiful blood, rich with the determination, the songs, the hope, the heartbreak, and the strength of my people, stretching back past the cocoon of my childhood home in Augusta, Georgia, beyond the most storied of concert halls, beyond the earth's surface, beyond, even, the nurturing glow of the African sun. Because they were, I am.
>
> JESSYE NORMAN, *Stand Up Straight and Sing! A Memoir*

ALICIA: I think about the heat. All the energy flowing through our cells, and how we are linked to our ancestors only by life and breath in an unbroken chain of life from the beginning when a woman delivers a child into the world, a cycle that keeps repeating, insistently, life to life to life to life. Unbroken. Isn't that amazing? To me this is a little like the performance of songs over and over. They are alive. They are still just passed from one person to another, and when they are performed they are alive. The thought of Jessye Norman traveling the world singing these songs makes me think of a sort of pollination. And so she just has "children" everywhere. Having grown up with her records in my ear, I know that I am one.

//

JASON: Early in his career Berg wrote his cycle of *Seven Early Songs* for voice and piano. He played piano. Thirty years later, he was in demand as a composer and decided to revisit this song cycle and orchestrate it. Berg's sense of melody and harmony is slippery, movable, and full of gravity. The strings snake around the melody. The strings often glide down as Jessye Norman's voice ascends. . . . A perpetual back and forth makes us feel like we're spinning until the soprano reaches the top: "Die Rosen aufgesprungen!" ("The roses have sprung up!")

This phrase reappears at the end of the song, too, and this time Berg ties the knot, totally resolves it with the most straightforward major triad at the end, and there it rests. Berg composed this song while falling in love with his wife Helene Berg.

ALICIA: This *is* a song for the night. There's a majestic, mysterious quality . . .

JASON: . . . those shifting harmonies . . . and we go through all these tonal movements with Alban and Jessye during the piece and when we reach the final exhalation, we've earned it.

All this maneuvering within Berg's structure and with poetic metaphors in German Romantic style makes me wonder about Jessye and her home soil in Georgia. What would it mean to her to send and sing songs around the world? And what does it mean to be a poet with your work reimagined as song?

ALICIA: All three, Performer, Composer, and Poet, enter new soil together every time an audience listens. Music has that power to stitch lives to other lives without so much as blinking, in that way. I can set a poem written 100 years ago to notes I am hearing in the present day. This is allowed, and this feels good to us. The poet is long passed away and new songs are allowed to be made, are welcomed to be made. The standards are rearranged over and over again. Rearrangements of all the evidence.

In her hand a summer hat,
Bearing in silence the sun's heat,
Not knowing what to do.

To hear Jessye amid all this is to hear vocalic harmony, echoes of a voice inside the same voice. Inner galactic reaches manifest stars that shine and then fall back, fall into her mouth. We want to be swallowed up whole. In rapture—through the dynamic of time, the dimension of travel and motion, of escape with intentional velocity—and in rhythm.

We sing to the emotion and not to the noun. To what "Nachtigall" with dark [a] and with [x] makes us feel, and not just what it is.

//

It is because the nightingale
Has sung throughout the night,

That from the sweet sound
Of her echoing song
The roses have sprung up.

JASON: Upon the death of Jessye Norman in 2019, Alicia and I revisited Jessye's performances of Alban Berg's *Seven Early Songs.* We stopped at "Die Nachtigall." In less than two minutes and twenty-two seconds, Jessye somehow took us through a lifetime.

Listeners think about their own history. Each eardrum is shaped as distinctly as any fingerprint.

As a pianist, I have a piano to touch. I can hear the soundboard feed the sound back to me as I press the keys. But for Alicia, the instrument is in her body. It has to vibrate the core in a way that I can't imagine.

Not knowing what to do.	Und weiß nicht, was beginnen.

Das macht, es hat die Nachtigall
Die ganze Nacht gesungen;
Da sind von ihrem süssen Schall,
Da sind in Hall und Widerhall
Die Rosen aufgesprungen.

11 "Wusuli Boat Song" / "Water Is Wide": History of a Cross-Cultural Duet

ABIGAIL WASHBURN AND WU FEI

In the Year of the Snake, two girls were born on opposite sides of the planet.

[Wú Fēi, FEI] I was born at the Fuxing Hospital in the Xicheng District in Beijing, China, 1977. My mother labored for two days alone in a small hospital room afraid she was going to die. My father was not allowed to enter.

[Abigail Washburn, ABBY] I was born in Evanston, Illinois, 1977. My mother did not even know she was in labor until my head popped out when she went to the bathroom, and minutes later I was born on the welcome mat of the St. Francis Hospital across the street. My dad says I flew out like a football and he caught me like a quarterback.

//

WE: We didn't know that thirty years later we would be sitting on a porch together in Nashville, Tennessee, weaving together songs from our home countries.

ABBY: The hardest time in my life came after my first child, Juno, was born in 2013. After eleven hours of hard labor, his little body whooshed in the water of a birthing tub at Vanderbilt Hospital, he was put to my breast, and his instinctual suckling began. I did not know how to hold this baby close enough. The weight of responsibility rocked me into a fog of postpartum depression that took years to leave me be. At two and a half months my husband and I began to tour, playing five to six shows a week when on the road. We discovered Juno had FPIES when we first tried to feed him baby oats in a green room in Indiana. Several episodes of heaving enterocolitis and he would not open his mouth to a spoon again until he was two years old. The instinctual suckling became his lifeline all night and all day. I was afraid he would die. I needed sleep.

FEI: The hardest moment of my life was when my first child, Viola, was born in 2012. She came into the world with a birth defect called TE fistula. She had to have a surgery fifteen hours after birth at the Beijing United Family Hospital, where she spent the first seven weeks of her life fighting to live. I barely held her after I gave birth. The next time I saw her was when she was being pushed into the operation room. I remember hearing the endless footfalls of my husband, Jeremy, as he pushed me in the wheelchair to the waiting room on the operation floor. I felt like I was the main character in a horror movie I must have seen before—quiet terror filled the air: I knew that my daughter might not come out of that room alive. After a month and a half of battling, Viola made a full recovery. The doctors and nurses called it a miracle.

WE: We sat together on the porch in Nashville on a September day, the air still thick from a southern summer. We understood the lush and tired green of the trees surviving another Tennessee August.

"What are the lullabies you sing? What puts Juno to sleep?"

"There is a version of an old Scottish folk song called 'The Water Is Wide,' about a mother and her child."

> The water is wide, I can't cross o'er
> And neither have I wings to fly
> Give me a boat that can carry two
> And we shall row, my child and I.

FEI: Abby started to sing words with long held notes and a melody with a slow rise and fall, like a wide curved river across the plains. I could hear the bendy meandering of a melody, a lilting lullaby from my own childhood. It was "Wusuli Boat Song" from the Hezhe people in northeast China. There is a dwindling population of some 10,000 Hezhe. They live their lives on boats on the Wusuli River, rocking back and forth to the bends and curves of the waves and the river.

<table>
<tr><td>乌苏里乌拉,</td><td>Wusuli river flowing on my land,</td></tr>
<tr><td>纳尼哟纳贝</td><td>Vast mountains, blue water,</td></tr>
<tr><td>绵绵的青山，蓝蓝的水</td><td>Fish shoot, waves fly,</td></tr>
<tr><td>鱼儿那个窜呐，浪儿那个飞</td><td>Mama stands on the boat front,</td></tr>
<tr><td>额涅在船头她摇着宝贝</td><td>rocking her baby to sleep.</td></tr>
</table>

FEI: There is an interesting fact about the beginnings of the two songs: they both start with a melodic interval of a "perfect fourth" ascending, which can help us see this shared human emotion of "longing." "Amazing Grace," Robert Schumann's "Träumerei," "L'Internationale"—these all begin with a perfect fourth. One thing all these songs share is that they open a hopeful place in the heart. The combination of "Wusuli Boat Song" and "Water Is Wide" is an inevitable reflection of the stage of life that Abby and I were living in—staying strong and hopeful for our children and ourselves as working mothers for the first time.

The second interesting fact is the different pitch ranges of the two songs. In "Water Is Wide," the entire melody stays within one octave sung slowly legato throughout the song. In contrast, the melody of "Wusuli Boat Song" is much busier, covering more vocal registers. Most of its phrases span the interval of a twelfth from highest to lowest (e.g., from A down to D). One phrase even reaches a minor thirteenth (from D down to F-sharp), a vocal span not often found in folk music.

ABBY: "Water Is Wide" sounds like a peaceful ocean, slowly and methodically increasing its melodic range within a single octave. The crest of the wave only reaches its highest point three-quarters of the way through the verse.

Meanwhile, the melody of "Wusuli Boat Song" jumps from the highest pitch to the lowest pitch in the first instant, just like the impossibly curvy Wusuli River itself. Our landlocked human perspective can blind us from knowing the truth that all water comes from and returns to the same source.

I can't pinpoint the first time I heard "The Water Is Wide," but it seeped into my American consciousness at a very young age. I know this because I can't remember a time when I didn't know the melody, or the idea that the water can be wide.

FEI: Similarly, "Wusuli Boat Song" is a song that I have known since I had memory in China. It was one of the most popular songs sung everywhere on Chinese TVs and radios. There was singing in almost every household in China. Karaoke was hugely popular there. Ironically, as a child, singing folk and pop songs on a karaoke machine was an escape for me from practicing music too much. When I was five, my parents decided that I should take instrument lessons. They invited two professors from China Conservatory of Music to our home. The professors gave me a thorough exam on whether I would be qualified to study music. They checked the bone structure on my fingers and tested my pitches and rhythms when singing and clapping what I had heard. I passed the exam. From that day, music has become my lifelong partner. I started taking guzheng lessons every week with a minimum of two hours of practice every day. Under this regimen, it didn't take long for my love of music to disappear. As an only child, I carried the responsibility not only to achieve the highest level academically, but also to fulfill the dreams my parents were not allowed to follow when they were young and the country was in political chaos.

ABBY: Fei told me that she was trained to be a musical soldier. From the youngest age, she spent hours upon hours every day behind the instrument, alone with the strings and picks and sheet music rather than in the Hutong alleys and playgrounds with other children.

I was not trained to be a professional musician. I always loved to sing in choirs, but when I tried out for lead roles, I never got them. I played the recorder for two years in fourth and fifth grades. I played the piano for two years until my teacher wouldn't let me learn music by ear and I quit. I played the flute for a year in the eighth grade after finding one at a garage sale. I thought I might look pretty if I had a flute. My parents encouraged music but did not force it. My longing to get involved in humanitarian causes far outweighed my interest in music. My mom said I carried the weight of the world on my shoulders.

FEI: The friendship and understanding between Abby and me grew not only from working together, but also from being mothers. Raising families and keeping careers going were tough. Our friendship went through ups and downs as we became closer, just like any relationship in life. Our drastically different backgrounds in music made me feel frustrated at times when we worked together.

We came to our collaboration speaking two overlapping and powerful universal musical languages: one that emphasizes traditions of the notated style of classical music and the other that draws on a venerable history of aural and improvised creativity. These "languages" or "dialogical approaches" share much in common; for example, they both aim to achieve the same kind of inspirational uplift. One of the big differences in our musical upbringing is the fact that classically trained musicians like myself are taught to read music from the first lesson, because notation is the primary musical language used in schools and private lessons around the world going back many hundreds of years. Folk musicians, on the other hand, traditionally learn music by ear, which has resulted in countless mild alterations to folk songs over generations. This makes it one of the most fascinating musical traditions, because one song can take on so many forms over long periods of time.

Many musicians have discussed the pros and cons of each of these approaches and traditions until they're blue in the face, and as you can imagine, these differences caused some obvious challenges in our approach to making music together. But we always managed to find solutions. For example, my ability to learn new music not just from reading notation but also from listening and memorizing became better and better. Through working together with synergistic empathy, we built up a syntax and vocabulary that allowed us to maintain our own musical voices while also enabling us to find a unique harmony together. Our careers kept growing stronger as a pair.

Our personal lives have grown stronger together as well, and our children have become best friends.

ABBY: Viola fell and hurt her lip one time when she was playing with Juno in our living room. I jumped to help her. Fei in a relaxed state said that after what Viola went through she was the toughest little girl in the whole world.

FEI: Theodore is Abby and Béla's second son. In a way, he is like one of my own. One evening, a few months after Theodore was born, I was putting my children to bed. A text message from Abby popped up on my phone. "Theodore is in the hospital now. He's not feeling well. He's been bleeding out of his mouth.... Please send your strength...." My heart must have stopped for a few seconds. The feeling I had was exactly like when I was told about Viola's situation after I gave birth to her. I knew Abby needed help that night, badly. My children luckily had fallen asleep, and I exchanged a few messages with Abby about where Theodore was hospitalized. Vanderbilt Children's Hospital was big. I finally found the right floor following the directions Abby had given me. It was already late at night. Walking in the hallway of all the wards filled with sick children, I instantly felt I was back in the moment when I was being pushed on a wheelchair to see Viola before her surgery. The lights, the walls, the tiled floors, the smell and the beeping sounds of all the medical equipment, all the nurses who work on night shifts, the intense, scary, and endless quietness in the air ... I had been there once. When I arrived in Theodore's room, a few friends were already there with Abby and Béla. Everyone looked exhausted and worried. Theodore was being held down in bed with people taking turns applying pressure to his wound to try to stop the endless bleeding. "Oh my god, I've been there before!" I thought. It is every mother's worst nightmare—not being able to do anything to make your child feel better when the child is sick.

After a week of struggling in the hospital, Theodore came home. However, he still takes medication every day. The strength and determination from his mother will cure him. That's what happened to me and my child.

Our Instruments

FEI: Both the guzheng and banjo are plucked string instruments. The banjo is originally from West Africa, and the guzheng has been around for 2,500 years. Both instruments have had a long history and witnessed much of humanity. Guzheng has a wide range of four octaves. In "Water Is Wide" and "Wusuli Boat Song," it is used rather more like a double bass to create a foundation that would embrace all the sounds within its natural reverberation.

ABBY: Contrary to popular belief in the United States, the banjo is not the spontaneous creation of southern white hillbilly culture. The five-string banjo is the western-industrialized long-lost grandchild of the grandmother akonting from the Gambia and Senegal. Much like the oppressed African slaves with whom it traveled to America, it was cut off from its heritage. Homemade akontings, made on American soil with bits of wood, gourd, and hide from its new environment, became the banjo at plantation dances. The banjo met the fiddle on the dance floor, the trance-like groove and subtle melodies of the banjo met the robust melodies from Scotland, Ireland, and England, and a new American sound was born. This sound is associated with the beginnings of blues, old-time bluegrass, country, and jazz. This music tradition is no doubt among America's greatest inventions in modern times, and it is the result of the oral traditions passed along through the natives, the slaves, and the immigrants who chose or were forced to bless our shores with this amazing melding of sound.

For "The Water Is Wide," I play an open-back five-string banjo, most commonly associated with old-time frailing or clawhammer style. However, I do not play it in clawhammer style on this song. Instead I use the slow-moving open ring of a three-finger picking style, using just the flesh of the tips of my fingers to pull on the metallic strings, softening a potentially more brittle sound that would otherwise be made with the sound of metallic finger picks. This can create a feeling of continuously rolling waves. I play most of the chords with this forward roll, except for one with a minor sixth, for which I switch to a backward two-finger roll only playing the top three strings of the banjo, emphasizing the upper register and adding space and sparkle at a moment of darker tonal color.

There is no Suzuki Method for the banjo. Every player must forge their own path. They can find a teacher, they can find a tablature book, they can listen to recordings and try to play what they hear, they can just sit and hold the instrument and see what comes. I've heard it said, even in the mountains where the tradition of old-time banjo grew its more recent roots, "Every holler has its own style." The banjo gives the musical gift of imperfect dissemination and of endless possibility.

FEI: The guzheng is a five-foot-long, twenty-one-string Chinese zither with about 2,500 years of history. It remains very popular in China since the earliest times. The guzheng is plucked mostly with finger picks attached to most of the fingers on both hands, and it is often tuned in the pentatonic scale. Much of the world's music is in the pentatonic scale, each tradition offering its own flavor. There are many schools of guzheng playing from different regions and different gurus. Changing gurus is considered betrayal in traditional Chinese art forms. So it was a traumatic experience for my parents when they realized I had outgrown my first guru. They had to find a new guru who could usher me to the next musical level but, sadly, at the expense of dishonoring my first guru. We were all freaked out. Looking back, I just wish my first guru could have recognized when I was pushing beyond what she had to offer and led me to the next place, but this is not the culture, and thus it is an impossibility. Many of my friends in the conservatory had very similar experiences. The ancient saying describes it as 一日之师，终身为父—"one day of a teacher, father for a lifetime." When I came to the States in 2000, I learned for the first time that students were encouraged to change professors every semester so they could study different perspectives.

Ironically, the one thing that I brought with me to America was my guzheng, which once was like shackles on my hands and spirit, and now has become my cherished life partner.

WE: String instruments from all over the world sound good when they are played together. The combination of the guzheng and banjo is no exception. The banjo sounds like ocean waves, steadily moving forward, while the guzheng creates at times a waterfall-like glissando and other times with a single pluck on the low strings can sound like an orchestral gong. Different plucking patterns counterpoint organically on the two instruments throughout songs like "The Water Is Wide" or the "Wusuli Boat Song."

Our Songs

ABBY: "The Water Is Wide" has passed through many sources on its journey to contemporary suburban America. It is the song of immigrants of Scotland and Ireland, an English export, a song passed along in the oral tradition of the eastern seaboard of the United States, and now a song that finds a home in many cultures around the world. In most iterations, with floating verses gathered from many centuries, it is known as a song of romantic love, unrequited love, or love waning with time. As it has passed through hands and voices, it has taken on different verses, different meanings. For some, it is a song of longing to be with one's God. "The Water Is Wide" was passed to me as a story of the courage of a mother who folds her child into herself and rows on.

FEI: "Wusuli" is one of the most loved folk songs in China and originated with the Hezhe people, an ethnic group who have one of the smallest populations. As a kid, I always thought it was a Han folk song. I am a Han. The Han make up more than ninety percent of mainland China's population. A famous Han tenor made this song widely known in the 1950s. He took credit as the songwriter of "Wusuli Boat Song." Much later in my life, I discovered that this song is from the Hezhe. Only about a decade ago, the Hezhe people won a lawsuit and took authorship of the melody of "Wusuli Boat Song" back from this singer. I always wonder—how many folk songs out there are still under the shadow of untruthful representation and appropriation?

WE: The folk songs we love are the ones we heard around us: from family and friends, teachers, recordings by collectors, community members, elders. Our separate enthrallment with the folk music of our native cultures is what led us to one another. A song passed through the ages from old Scotland to a Nashville suburb, a song passed from the Hezhe people of northern China to a Han girl in the hutongs of Beijing ... and now ours is a song weaving them together. Is it an awe-inspiring feat of geography and time or just the way a river moves, a wave rolling ever rhythmically toward its universal home?

Our Singing

WE: Our voices have their own strong and different characters. We do not sound like each other at all when we sing alone. Fei's voice likes to sit in the soprano range, traveling on a high cloud, whipping itself along with a piercing forward float, while Abby's voice sits more in the alto range, living less in the head and more in the chest, sometimes gritty and rough around the edges but also soft and comforting.

When we sing together, our distinct voices and singing styles create a new combination, the highs drawing the lows upward, the lows preparing a landing place for the falling highs. We don't have to sound similar to harmonize. Not at all. And that is a truth of the world we live in, which we rarely see or appreciate—the power of difference is to create beauty.

12 "Loud Dreaming": Of Mothers and Sisters and Lessons in Listening

DAPHNE A. BROOKS

In memory of T.M., our literary ambassador of Black radical sound

In loud dreaming, monologue is no different from a shriek.

TONI MORRISON, *Paradise*

Out at the edge of the universe she is inventing her own philosophies that take the form of heartbreaking laments. She records repressed histories that run the length of gorgeously disobedient vocal runs. She stands in the wilderness of her own design, the frontier upon which she is busy making maps sewn together with the delicacy of her rich and varied phrasings, the kind that evoke the landscape of our oft-forgotten, our overlooked, our taboo and unregulated desires. A renegade storyteller, a dramatic sonic actor, a sly comedian, and a dreamy romance heroine, Cécile McLorin Salvant is the kind of artist who breaks all sorts of rules in the storied jazz tradition—while yet still remaking it for a new generation. She is for me as well the sonic analogue to Dame Toni Morrison's vast and prodigious literary archive. Salvant's vertiginous song cycle *Ogresse*, a gothic parable that she first unfurled in 2018 at New York's Museum of Modern Art, is a dizzying masterpiece, weird and unsettling, both luminous and haunting. It knocked the wind out of me the first time I saw her perform it there, since to me it felt like one epically long song, the manifestation of all of the music that Morrison, that colossus of American letters, had translated into stirring language across a career that spanned nearly half a century. *Ogresse* was music in the form of a compressed, seventy-five-minute one-woman jazz opera of sorts, a compendium of the sounds that our *Beloved* author often described hearing in her parents' home while growing up in thirties and forties Lorain, Ohio.

A robust and varied musicality was, according to Morrison, pivotal and informative, a thing of awe and beauty to her as a child, and her reflections on this topic in interviews and lectures always stuck with me, since the stratified nature of my own family—much older parents, much older siblings—meant that the music archive in our home stretched across generations, beginning with Basie's meticulous swing, looping through the buoyancy of Motown and the bacchanalia of disco, and landing in my own punk and New Wave teen world of disaffected cool. On this score, I found in her unlikely kin. Born Chloe Ardelia Wofford in 1931, Morrison also absorbed the sounds of her family members. All had musical talents that, as she was quick to point out, were not to be hers. "I was surrounded by all kinds of music as a girl," she described in an *Opera America* lecture that she delivered in 2005. "All the adults in my family, it seemed, could play instruments when they picked them up. None of them could read music, but all of them could hear music and then repeat it." Their craft and artistic communions were ubiquitous and especially resonant in the figure of her mother, a gifted vocalist who "completely dominated" young Morrison's sonic world. "My mother sang opera," she would often recount, "she sang sentimental Victorian songs, she sang arias from *Carmen*, she sang jazz, she sang blues, she sang what Ella Fitzgerald sang. . . ." The variety and virtuosity of her mother's interpretative range went unmatched in the Wofford household. "She sang," Morrison would add in the 2004 preface to her sixth novel, *Jazz*, "the way other people muse. A constant background drift of beautiful sound I took for granted, like oxygen. 'Ave Maria, gratia plena . . . I woke up this morning with an awful aching head / My new man has left me just a room and a bed . . . Precious Lord, lead me on . . . I'm gonna buy me a pistol, just as long as I am tall. . . . L'amour est un oiseau rebel. . . . When the deep purple falls over hazy garden walls . . . I've got a disposition and a way of my own / When my man starts kicking I let him find a new home. . . . . Oh, holy night. . . .' Like the music that came to be known as Jazz, she took from everywhere, knew everything . . . and made it her own." Such sonic philosophizing suggested cultural depth and enormity that to her had no equal. "So," she would add in her lecture with a bit of a wink, "my sister and I chose other routes." But Toni Morrison would carry her mother's imprint with her throughout her legendary career. For this very volume and before she took ill, she had planned to offer a meditation on the songs sung by her mother.

Consider this, then, a gathering ground of sorts where the legacies of both Salvant and Morrison take shape in the thunder and beauty of Salvant's long song expression of jazz alterity. For me, Salvant's sonic dreamwork is the manifestation of all of the wonder and possibility coursing through Morrison's reflections on scenes of intimate, familial musicality unfolding between parent and child. And so I imagine myself listening on two planes: envisioning the wisdom and instruction imparted from mother to daughter in musical language that spans genres and time periods, emotional complexity, and spiritual questioning and, likewise, traveling the span of Salvant's gripping performance, which approximates the topical, formalistic, and aesthetic magnitude of Toni Morrison's memory of her mother's music.

I was one of the lucky ones who experienced Salvant's song cycle *Ogresse* on two separate occasions in fall 2018 at New York City's Metropolitan Museum and one year later at Jazz at Lincoln Center's Rose Hall. In both instances, it was a performance that had me riveted and left me unmoored. A dark fairy tale spanning the marvelous and the tragic, the sensual as well as the brutal, *Ogresse* is a meditation on the alienating ways that human beings make and also destroy worlds with one another. The intoxicating charm that Salvant's grand, swirling suite initially conjures is a Trojan horse for the brutality that lies at the heart of this ominous parable, one that centers the emotional and eventually the physical desolation of a social outcast. This is the kind of Black girl sorrow warranting big music that speaks in many affective tongues.

One hears this in its epic scope. *Ogresse* is the sound of the multitudes of which Ramah Wofford's daughter speaks whenever she would detail her mother's artistic genius. Salvant, the daredevil vocalist, called by *New York Times* critic Nate Chinen the "finest jazz singer to emerge in the last decade," performs this original work—with lyrics of her own making and orchestrations by Darcy James Argue—by invoking an amalgamation of signature styles:

Fitzgerald-era swing and American songbook, classical music vocalizing and classic blues women's lament, cabaret chanson and midcentury musical theater, folk intimacy and earnestness as well as experimental bebop howl. It is a capacious sonic rendering of Morrison's own multiplicity of aesthetic registers, and like her work, it cleaves to the kind of rigorous ethical explorations that Morrison brought to each one of her eleven formidable and demanding novels. In *Ogresse*, then, we arrive at the place where a mother's music and a daughter's fiction that was shaped, in part, by her mother's artistic example, come full circle. Salvant has, in effect, and by way of this work, collaborated in composing a Toni Morrison songbook of sorts—a sublime, one-woman jazz romance with an unsettling, Brothers Grimm–like underbelly that, just as Morrison's novels always do, forces its audience to confront the widespread and corrosive impact of racial and gender subjugation permeating the very foundation of American culture.

//

People tell me that I am always writing about love. . . . In fact, I am always writing about betrayal. Love is the weather. Betrayal is the lightning that cleaves and reveals it.

TONI MORRISON, *Love*

We are there for the fall. It is a nuanced, aching spiral downward, one that has a different emotional tenor to it than that of the heartbreak of Billie or Sarah or Dinah, all masters of deeply revelatory blues and jazz women's angst that manages to compress the gestation period of entire relationships down to pregnant phrasings (in the case of Holiday), glissandos that swoop with longing (as is true of Vaughan), or worldly restraint (one of Washington's signature moves). A student of this illustrious vocal history, Salvant always wears her intelligence of this important archive of sounds on her sleeve. But *Ogresse*, one of those all-too-rare occasions in which women jazz artists are given room to create whole fictive landscapes in which to roam, marks the emergence of a protagonist in the genre whose evolution and development reaches back to an idyllic past ("I was born in a redwood / house in the clouds") and stretches all the way to her violent demise, consumed by passion and poisoned by the consumption of love itself. The tragedy is Shakespearean in its basic plot turn as the title character and the lover whom she believes to have betrayed her ultimately perish and "travel together / to that undiscovered country / from which no one ever returns. . . ."

//

*There is a difference between being put out and being put out*doors.

TONI MORRISON, *The Bluest Eye*

Salvant's take on this narrative convention, however, is exhaustive in its sonic originality, a wholly Black feminist reinterpretation of age-old folkloric myths that traffic in "beauties" and "beasts," in the aspirations of supposed "prince charmings" and the dreams of "lily-white" damsels in distress. Like much of Morrison's body of work, *Ogresse* is a tale of root-and-branch betrayal that starts in the home where the waltzing sumptuousness of a mother's love (a figure who held our protagonist "to the sky . . . and sang songs of [her] beauty") is swiftly displaced by the rule of an abusive stepfather who "tried to put" our girl "into his mouth." What unfolds is an origins tale, the birth of her fantastic "monstrosity," as Salvant refers to it, which also becomes a source of her survival ("I bit his head off / and then I fled off into the woods"). This is the forebodingly gothic story of what it means to be "outdoors," the situation in which, as Morrison puts it in her first novel, "there is no place to go. . . . the end of something, an irrevocable, physical fact, defining and complementing" of one's "metaphysical condition. . . ."

What's astonishing is the dramaturgical might that she brings to this tale of existential crisis. With speed and precision, Salvant bobs and weaves between Ogresse's first-person narration, the voice of her wolf-in-sheep's-clothing suitor, and that of a third-person narrator conveying the details of the tragedy as it unfolds. And I remain enraptured by the ways that she mines her heroine's fortress of solitude, drawing out the micro-feelings of her hesitancy to succumb to love. I'm dazzled, too, by the power she exudes when inhabiting the words and posturing of a villain-turned-swooning-admirer, dissecting the enemy's emotional anatomy from the inside out, wrapping him in increasingly feminized expressions of longing that unfurl across lush string arrangements.

Just as Morrison does in her novels, Salvant carefully moves these characters like pieces on a chessboard as she pushes toward cataclysm in this tale of suffering, expulsion, and othering fueled by the spectacle of her heroine's racial difference. Everything you need to know about the sheer depth and fearless invention of Cécile McLorin Salvant's musicianship can, in fact, be found in a cutting refrain that threads through the middle section of her performance. "I do not believe you" are the lyrics she first delivers thirty-six minutes into the song cycle. It is an initial response to a man on a fool's errand, one whose pursuit of a bounty to slay the supposed "black beast" of the woods leads him to dispassionately woo her with the jaunt and confidence of a suave, supper club serenade. "I do not believe you," sings Salvant's heroine in response to his declaration of her beauty, "why should I believe you?" Four times she turns over this pronouncement of incredulity, wringing each version of the phrase for subtle, explosive shifts in her character's emotional ontology—from halting disbelief, to softening inquisition, and finally to faltering submission that is laced with fear, "*what* if I believe you?"

This is the ethical current that runs through Salvant's work and Morrison's many masterpieces as well. It is the line of questioning that pays homage to our magnificent author's moral imagination in that it ponders the intimacies of oppression, the risks of surrendering to those who hold power over you, the truth and falsities informing the ability to forge trust with another. "Why should I believe you? What if I believe you?" sings Ogresse to the townsman who expediently professes his adoration for her. What will happen if I give up the terms of my self-possession? Why shouldn't I "refuse the thing that's been refused to me"? Like a Morrison heroine faced with new and uncertain peril, like Sethe in *Beloved* confronting the return of a wounded and malevolent baby ghost, like Heed and Christine, who, in *Love*, are forced to confront the wreckage of the patriarch who ravaged each of their lives, like Violet in *Jazz,* who reels from her husband's infidelity, like Florens in *A Mercy,* who falls head-over-heels for a freeman who ultimately desecrates the meaning of her freedom, Salvant's Ogresse contemplates the terms of her own self-possession as well as the credibility of her oppressor.

She also imparts a set of questions that, for any Black feminist listener, exceed the boundaries of that character's perilous seduction, and the hypnotic repetition of these questions at two key junctures in the performance whispers to us the Morrisonian key to our own liberation: reject the racial and gender shibboleths that banish a girl from her own household, that insist to her, as Ogresse comes to believe, that "blackness" is a thing to be expunged from the face of the earth, that "whiteness," in the form of the wandering-in-the-woods girl "Lily," is precious and prized. Reject the patriarchal ruses that "set things up" this way and, instead, fundamentally question the epistemological tyranny of a world in which blackness and womanhood are easily and brutally disregarded and seemingly *must* be discarded for the presumptive sanctity of communities.

The tragedy that befalls Salvant's heroine is one in which such an awakening comes at great cost. If early on her protagonist poses the question "Who's gonna love / a big black beast like me?" in the middle of the otherwise insouciant romp that is "I'm Breezy," the subsequent brutal twists to that question's answer convey the depths of cruelty in the world that she inhabits. Yet the question itself foreshadows the radical musical transformation that emerges as *Ogresse* comes to a close. Salvant's refrain is potent and, by fits and starts, in the wake of Ogresse's discovery of having been duped, it is insistent in its heavy knowing and excess. One hour and seven minutes into our journey with her, her refrain takes its sharpest turn, gradually escalating, becoming a crescendo of fury. Here, jazz balladry transfigures into the very "sound of the riot." In this version of the refrain, "the lightning that cleaves and reveals" betrayal noisily announces itself. There is no turning back, and we are pulled into the heart of disaster. Though her hunter-turned-suitor is now sincerely in love, his initial lies stoke her "rage" as it becomes a "forest fire." This is the *Sturm und Drang*, the beginning of the end, the "circles and circles of sorrow" that have "no top" and "no bottom," the kind of ache that Morrison's characters know so well. We move from quiet, slow-simmering dirge, a funeral march led by melodica and organ, bass clarinet and mournful strings—the eventual full fourteen-member ensemble of players that periodically restates Ogresse's questions. They make a slow-growing wave of sound through the valley of fully realized sadness that erupts into an eloquent cacophony encapsulating our heroine's murderous resolve. We walk the line with them in a grim procession. The misery has arrived.

//

Had she paints, or clay, or knew the discipline of dance, or strings; had she anything to engage her tremendous curiosity and her gift for metaphor, she might have exchanged the restlessness and preoccupation with whim for an activity that provided her with all she yearned for. And like any artist with no art form, she became dangerous.

TONI MORRISON, *Sula*

But the heroine's ruin runs counter to the fugitive form of *Ogresse* itself. For it is its form, in fact, that remains the final statement, it would seem, on what this disruptive work is suggesting about the limitless originality of Black sonic womanhood forged in the crucible of historical marginalization and the chronic diminution of Black women's musical genius. *Ogresse* is a "wild" work, one that courses through so many sounds and yet lives outside of any one genre. Its orphic preface conjures the mood of a sonic fable; its cyclical interludes follow the folk rhythms of a picaresque banjo that beckons us to travel through the tensions in its storybook town; the Rat Pack cocktail culture misogyny of a song like "She's Big" ("she's bigger than a tree / she's vast / she's vaster than the sea / she opens her mouth / it's the size of a planet") finds its swing counterpoint in the rebellious "I'm Breezy" ("I'm happy, mostly / I do what I want / whenever I want / when Folks come laughing / and leering and pointing at me / I eat them for breakfast / with tea"). It delights in cabaret chansons that traffic in the racist caricature of colonial culture ("C'est très simple à faire / 700g de chair / fraîche de paysan . . . 100g de beurre") while yet still undoing such stereotypes by conveying the complex interiority of a Black heroine who is, at turns, a screwball "counterdiva," as Margo Jefferson has referred to Salvant, and a heart-wrenching romantic lead. Even the terms of heteronormative American songbook desire, the kind that Ella sings to us so well, are upended in this work when Ogresse is "beguiled" by wandering white Lily ("what is that? / Who is that? / Skin like milk / hair like silk . . . what is it about a white woman / that does me in so?"). To be enchanted by whiteness, as some of Morrison's key characters are in her first and last novels, foreshadows her eventual undoing. As she "tumbles to the depths" toward the devastating climax, Salvant reaches into her classically trained wheelhouse of vocals to offer yet another musical tongue, something of a hymnody that might capture the cosmic catastrophe unfolding all around us.

Unruly and unregulated, Salvant's *Ogresse* is as big and boundless as its doomed heroine. But in its vision of a pariah who strives and fails to attempt to live outside of the constrictions of the dominant and the proper, it dares to envision, as does Morrison's ninth novel, *A Mercy*, a kind of womanhood perched in the "wide and untrammeled space" of the forest frontier, away, for a spell, from the mob intent on annihilating her. There she might pursue her curiosity, outlive her restlessness, find the form that she might shape into her own exquisitely expressive conduit. Salvant gives us glimpses of this bold and other way of being, this wildness that is insistently defiant rather than deviant. There is another world, this song cycle seems to suggest, one beyond "the great hill covered in flowers . . . covered in snakes," where Salvant sings the martyred bones of Ogresse to rest.

For this burial, she invites us to do some "loud dreaming" with her as she brings to a close her extended Black feminist sonic monologue, this archive of the shrieks and sighs, the coos and wails, the sounds mellifluous and discordant, vernacular and liturgical, dangerous and soothing, regal and whimsical, cantankerous and solemn. Here, with heavy melisma, a run of vocal trills, and nearly three minutes of ardent lyrical, nearly shamanistic repetition, she holds vigil and sounds out the scale of this tragedy. It is the "sound that [breaks] the back of words," and it does not shy away from pointing its finger at the long dead and still here who fail to listen to all of this history of the dispossessed. It is a reclamation of all of what we might yet still hold precious in the immense musical lexicon handed down to us by our mothers . . . and our sisters too.

Coda: Sister Act

[B]efore they know color from no color, kin from stranger . . . they have found a mix of surrender and mutiny they can never live without.

TONI MORRISON, *Love*

Eleven a.m., Saturday morning, 1975, in Menlo Park, California, and it's all happening on the other side of my big sister's bedroom door, the gateway to a forbidden palace of sound and movement and energy and teen weekend boogie-down productions. This is the place where there are so many lessons to be learned, as everyone from rock critic Cameron Crowe to rock musician Dave Grohl will tell you. An older sister's bedroom is a shrine of pop culture wisdom and pedagogy where brilliant exercises in nesting and fandom have the space to run amok.

On the other side of the bedroom door, where *Seventeen* magazine issues are strewn across the bed, where posters of Barbarino and the Fonz are plastered across the walls, where the TV is turned down real low in anticipation of Don Cornelius's weekly, euphoric, kinesthetic, locomotive Black-is-Beautiful odyssey, is that special, Black girl magic sacred place which, if you were seven years old, as I was back then, you had to lobby some kinda hard to gain entrance, to secure a pass, as it were, and cross the velvet rope into that fanciful spot where the Philly horns are booming. The slow-drag boogie-woogie rhythm section is driving, the harmonies of my sister's beloved Luther Vandross–led backup ensemble, the "audible blackness" to this far-out sound, are both glorious and assertively world-making in volume, as if announcing a new sonic racial ecology on the horizon, the kind in which "freedom dreams" are made for the weary, the post–Civil Rights young gifted and Black who long for even newer worlds in which they might affirm both their P-Funk "freakishness" *and* their glam rock–loving selves (two entwined genres of sound if ever there were some).

In the mix of it all, there is a voice that sounds like nothing I've ever heard before—something rare in my sister's truly excellent record collection, she being my great, pedagogical cultural archive to whom I am forever indebted. "White and male" but also more than that, it is a voice that is sly and knowing, urgent and wise, sexy and wanting—all terms that, of course, would not be at my disposal in the first grade but terms that I now call upon in my middle-aged years to characterize the sound of jubilant strangeness thumping through the speakers of my sister's stereo. To hell if I know what any of these oh-so-arcane verses actually mean, these lines about "afro-Sheilas" and that great villain of every Black American household, "president Nixon." I had not yet been schooled on trans-Atlantic rock cabaret irony back then.

I just know and feel in my bones as I awkwardly struggle (and fail!) to keep up with my sister (the Greatest. Dancer. Ever.) that this voice, this supremely "English-alienated" and alien voice of David Bowie, is sanctioning my own, Ezra Jack Keats and Maurice Sendak-informed future, my personally curated "wildness," as my friends Jack Halberstam and Tavia Nyong'o might refer to it. This "plastic soul man" is singing and sounding out the soundtrack to the kinds of sharp, self-critical cultural transgressions that would enable my own black square-peggedness to continue to grow and flourish in new Jim Crow California, where bussing and school class tracking replaced the systemic injuries of full-scale legislated segregation. There he is, mysteriously swathed in bright stage lights and color in the accompanying *Young Americans* album poster that my sister has affixed to her bedroom wall.

He is sharing the "Fame" limelight with one of the greatest R&B, funk, and jazz ensembles of my girlhood, the band that had a horn section that could get my dear father to bob his head from side to side even on a bad day, a band so virtuosic that it was capable of both swinging deep funk Afrofuture grooves like "Fantasy" and "Getaway" and delivering Black Power mixtape love songs for the next generation like "Shining Star" and "Devotion" all in one set: the Maurice White–led band known affectionately as "the elements," Earth, Wind & Fire. There they are, all decked out in post-Godfather-of-Soul jumpsuits, posing for the camera as they tumbled together forever in motion. They are my sister's favorite band, the soundtrack that buoys her up on those most stressful days of fractious 1970s Bay Area high school integration experiment projects. For me, they are the sound of Black wonderland togetherness and cosmic affirmation, a distinctively and unapologetically Black insistence of the human, of Black pleasure and joy, of a better and freer world than even our parents had dreamt for us. Several weeks after my father died back in 2003, I was reminded of this as I sat with a friend and we turned on an episode of the dearly departed *Bernie Mac Show*, one that made use of a Maurice White, Verdine White, and Charles Stepney–penned classic, "That's the Way of the World."

"The song is my favorite by them," I wrote to my sister back in 2016 after both White and Bowie had passed away. "There's a *Bernie Mac* episode where the oldest niece gets her own bedroom for the first time after battling it out with her curmudgeon uncle. Did you see that one? He does this voice-over about coming to recognize how important a teen Black girl's space is and how blessed he is to be able to give her that space. His voice-over accompanies the sight of Vanessa falling in slow motion onto her bed as 'That's the Way of the World' plays. We hear Maurice and company calling together to the congregation: 'We've come together on this special day / to sing our message loud and clear / Looking back we've touched on sorrowful days / Future, past, they disappear . . .'" I remember "bawling uncontrollably," I said to my sister, and "thinking that THAT is the sound of post–Civil Rights childhood" in all its glory, all its possibility, all of its willful and ecstatic sense of entitlement to be the funky, audacious, glamorous, and hopeful young Americans that our parents wanted so desperately for us to have the freedom to be. "Free to be, you and me," I reminded her. All of those lessons were stored up in the music I surrendered to every childhood weekend in her room.

13 Interval/Notation

MAUREEN N. MCLANE

This was going to be an essay on Guillaume de Machaut inventor of the first wall of sound. This was going to be about a kind of open fifth you can't modulate your mind out of. A friend to whom I submitted. With whom I shared. I have loved some conductors not others and have been myself conducted and not only by myself. Is the conductor a dictator. Let us salute the Orpheus Chamber Orchestra. The submission to a world of co-created sound that kind of ecstasy I can get behind, beside myself, standing outside myself into you. Call it participation. Call it reciprocity the linguistic circuit become choral. The kinds of listening we do as sound resound. Every day we throw our voices some days they are notated and some hours we throw our throats at printed notes the staves catch. I would never be a good jazz singer the state judge said I was unsuited to the vocal jazz ensemble it was a matter of personality. Did he mean whiteness. Did he mean tightness. We were almost all white up there in the snowbelt oh the flat foot floogie with a floy floy. Where was Alice Coltrane. Where was my love. Where did our love go. We can love John Cage's "Lecture on Nothing" and Cecil Taylor's calling out of Cage on jazz. Whose silence. Whose silencing. Are these unmusical questions. Most musical most melancholy bird a nightingale is not that said Coleridge exasperated by Milton and Wallace Stevens never heard a nightingale though yes he several times said *blackbird.* Singing in the dead of night. Singing in the dead. Oh fly all your life. A floy floy. Is every poem a conversation poem manqué every concert a composition. Ruth Crawford Seeger transcribed and notated so precisely the Lomaxes' recordings of Black singers that they could not use those first transcriptions for their songbook; unplayable they were by the general and yet what fidelity what respect for the singers of tales. When I was sad in the '90s I didn't listen to Liz Phair I didn't listen to Nirvana I didn't listen to Belly or Lead Belly it was Górecki why. An orchestral business within the intestines of life. A tuning up toward. Some days one sounds through an inner voice barely audible. A specific interval closes Machaut's Mass, perfect and just and open, notated in a new style.

14 A Change Is Gonna Come

CARRIE MAE WEEMS

Music by Sam Cooke

A Song to Sing

A Bell to Ring

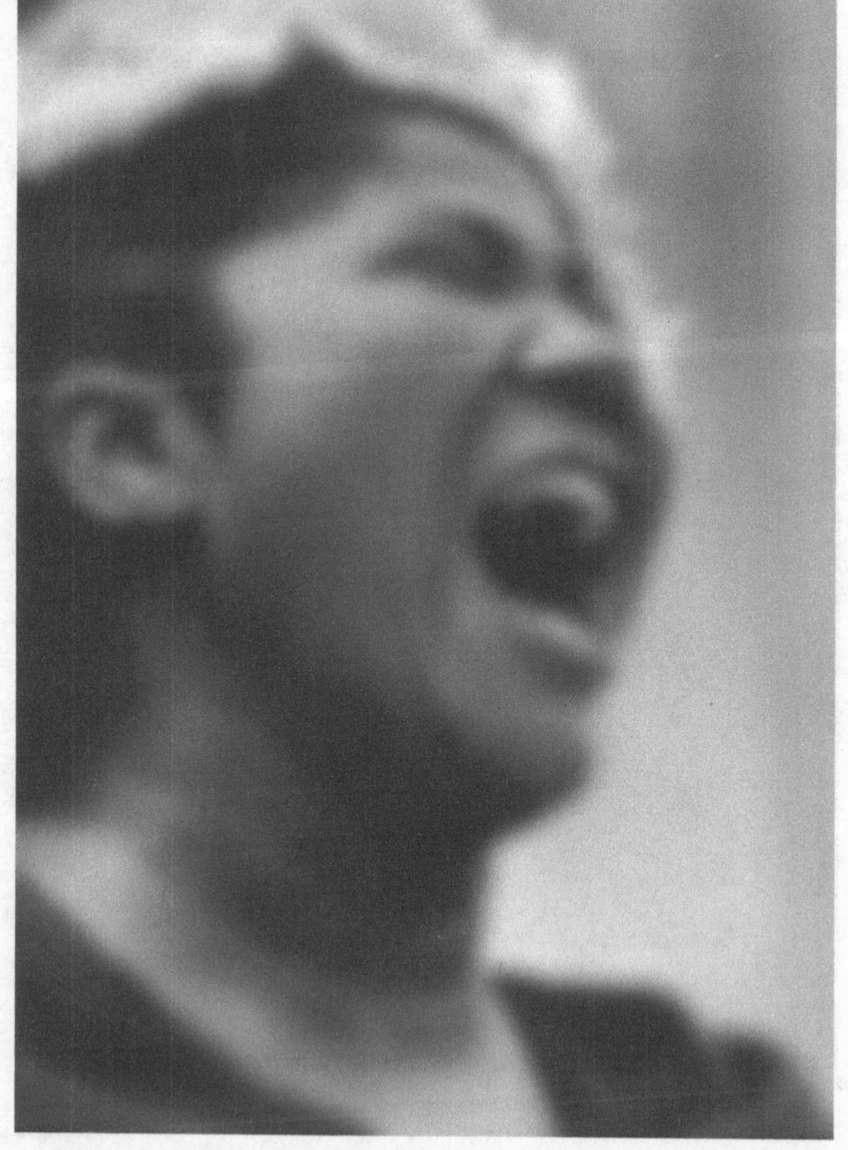

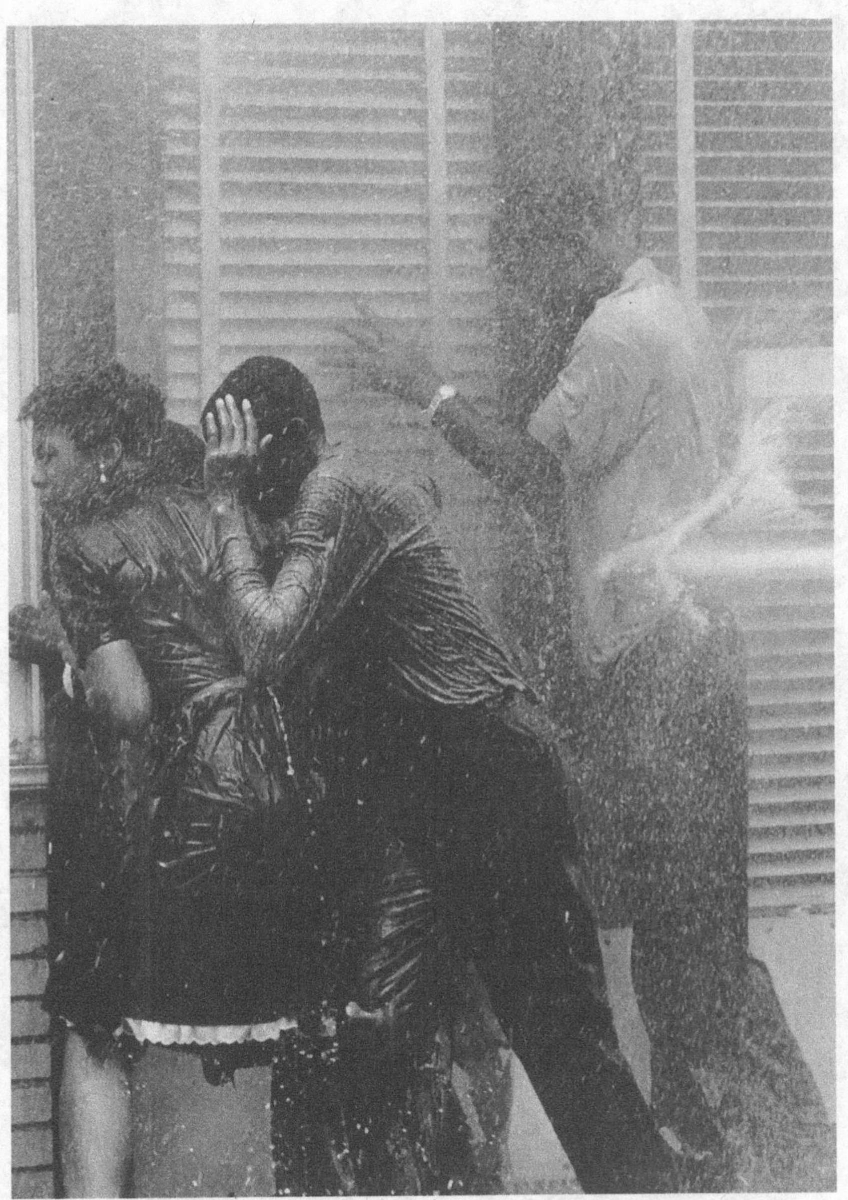

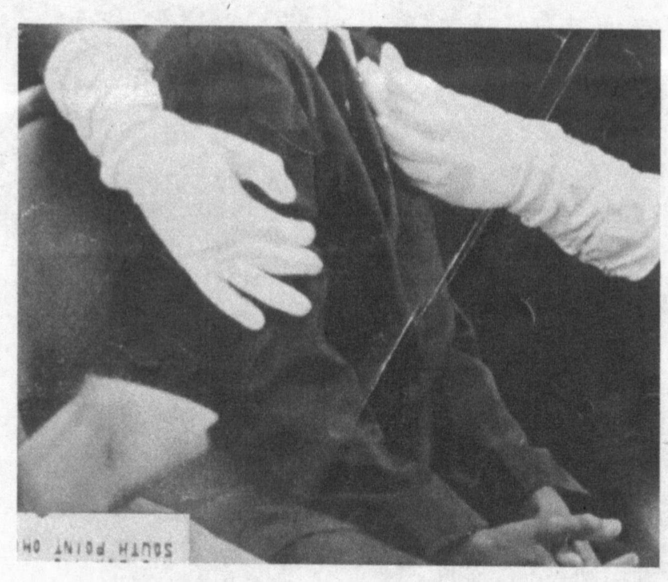
SOUTH POINT OH

PURPOSE

WASHINGTON

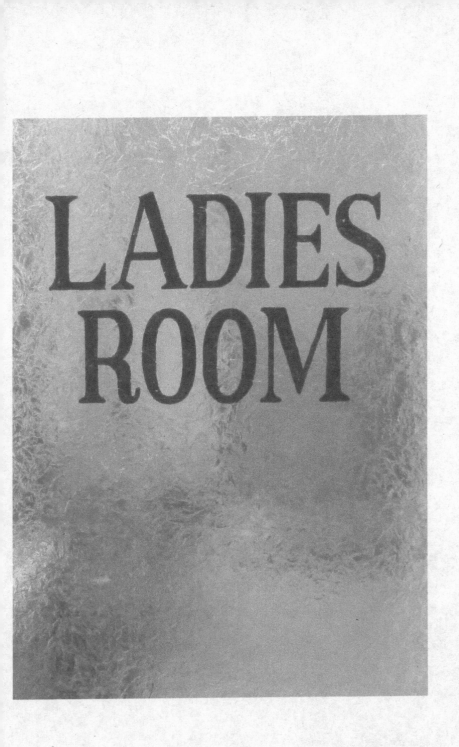

LADIES ROOM

It's been too hard living, but I'm afraid to die
'Cause I don't know what's up there, beyond the sky
It's been a long, a long time coming
But I know a change gonna come, oh yes it will

Lyrics by Sam Cooke

15 See the Music

BRIAN SEIBERT

When I took dance classes as a child, I was never the most flexible or technically polished student. Not even close. But my teachers would often single me out for being musical. I took that praise to mean that I was rhythmically precise, with an attentive, sensitive ear. I thought they were telling me that they could see how I heard the music in how I attempted to make my body move. That's what it felt like on the inside, anyway: like the point of dancing was to express the music as exactly as possible. That way, every motion felt supported, amplified, affirmed. It felt good.

Much later, when I became a dance critic, and was tasked with evaluating the musicality of dancers and choreographers, I began with much the same assumption: the more closely faithful to the music, the more "musical" the dance or dancer. Dances performed in silence or choreographed in a loose or ironic or aleatoric relationship to music soon complicated this notion. But even considering dances clearly intended to accord with a score, I grew to understand—through the process of trying to explain the effect that any combination of sound and motion had on me as a witness—that there was more to musicality than just mirroring.

Dance can make you hear differently. In one sense, to view a dance is to borrow the ears of the choreographer and the dancers. What you feel in your body while watching their bodies is their way of hearing. As with anything in art, any vision or interpretation, you're free to accept or reject it, in part or whole. But it's there. Often, at dance concerts, music is assumed to be secondary, to be accompaniment, down in the pit rather than up on stage, variously helping or hindering the dance. But it's fair to flip the question: how is this dance enhancing this music? I've found that the answer isn't always straightforward.

This is particularly true with canonical concert music. For a choreographer to select a great piece of music might seem a sensible decision, offering a firm foundation, even a crutch: at least *the music* will be great, and possibly some of that greatness might spread, or rub off, or flatter like designer apparel. At worst, viewers could always close their eyes and listen. No choreographer wants that, though, and so the selection of great music introduces the risk that the greatness of the music might expose the relative weakness of the dance. The stronger the music's architecture, the greater its invention and depth, the more the dance has to live up to. When Isadora Duncan started dancing to symphonies in the early twentieth century, some critics cried scandal and sacrilege. That was anti-dance prejudice, a presumption that dance can't touch certain music. That's not what I mean. There's nothing wrong with making a dance to Bach. I just mean that when I see Bach on a dance program, I might get a little nervous.

Imagine this. The music: the concluding allegro movement of Bach's beloved Concerto in D Minor for Two Violins. The choreography: a bunch of barefoot people sliding across the floor as if into home plate, or rolling around like tumbleweeds; men and women acting like children, stumbling, falling, running at full tilt and then leaping recklessly—with their landing-gear legs retracted, trusting that someone will catch them. *That* to *Bach?* Yes. This is the ending of Paul Taylor's dance *Esplanade*, and to me it doesn't just live up to Bach's score. I think it improves it.

I want to try to explain why, but first I want to point out an additional audacity. When Taylor choreographed *Esplanade*, in 1975, he knew that a much-revered dance set to the same piece of music already existed: George Balanchine's 1941 ballet *Concerto Barocco*. So in choosing that music, Taylor wasn't just taking on Bach; he was taking on Balanchine, too. This was bold. Balanchine, in 1975, was widely considered to be the greatest choreographer in the world. The core of Balanchine's mastery was acknowledged to be musical. Choosing the same piece of music was asking for tough comparisons.

Whatever Taylor's motivation, though, what he did in taking on that Bach score was help reveal something about the relationship between dance and music, something about how dance helps us hear. One musical masterpiece can match two wildly different masterpieces of choreography. Two choreographers can hear Bach in radically different ways and both be persuasive, both be "musical."

Of the two works, Balanchine's *Concerto Barocco* is the more obviously faithful to the score. Its title suggests that if it's about anything, it's about the music. The opening movement (Vivace) and the final one (Allegro) feature an ensemble of eight women fronted by two female soloists who seem patently to correspond to the two violins. Just as the two violinists take turns, trade phrases, echo, overlap, and intertwine, so do the two soloist dancers.

The correspondence isn't strict or formulaic, however. When the first violin introduces its theme, the first soloist dances alone, kicking forward with one leg, then backward with the other, those expansive weak-beat thrusts exactly reflecting both the shape of the melodic leaps and the slashing force of the violinist's unseen bow. And when the second violin enters, so does the second soloist, her inward twists and heel drops fitting the quieter, more intricate counterpoint. Yet this one-to-one identification doesn't hold. The ballerinas may be side by side and symmetrical, or revolve around one another as in a turnstile, or cross limb-swords tightly, almost jockeying for position. They have their own interplay, which complements that of the violins.

"See the music, hear the dance," a saying of Balanchine's, has become a slogan. The synesthetic idea of music and dance that he was getting at is commonly confused with simple music visualization, which is occasionally (and often dismissively) called "Mickey Mousing," after the illustrative way that movement and music are matched in cartoons. But the best and most musical choreographers don't do music visualization, not exactly.

A trained musician, Balanchine often spoke about music deferentially. He wrote that he was dependent on music not just for "the controlling image" of a dance, the inspiration, but for rhythms, which he said a choreographer can't invent, only reflect. "The organizing of rhythm on a grand scale," he wrote, "is a function of the musical mind," leaving out that his mind was musical. *Concerto Barocco* has its own logic, its own choreographic logic. Much as the orchestra, at the start of Bach's concerto, introduces musical material developed throughout the rest of the score, the dance ensemble introduces dance material that's repeated and varied. This includes specific steps, such as one that rises up and leans way off balance, or a sequence of three hops on pointe, and also broader physical themes: corkscrew action, a contrast between closed and open.

Often the playing out of these steps and themes links up with Bach's musical form, but Balanchine goes his own way, too. Sometimes, those tiptoe hops land smack on notes; other times, all that's underneath them, rhythmically, is an unstated pulse. In the central Largo movement, they sink softly into a descending line of exposed chords, their sinking deepening the music's slowing, and in the final movement, they go a little wild. Crowned with curved arms overhead, they're periodically punctuated with one arm dropping to meet an outstretched leg—which is exciting enough, but then the hopping women start dropping at different times, on different beats of the measure, and the stately bounce of Bach starts to feel syncopated, polyrhythmic, more like Stravinsky or jazz. It always makes me move in my seat.

After you watch that—*while* and after—you hear Bach differently, with Balanchine's ears. A choreographer really can help you see the music, notice things, as if the dancers were human highlighters illuminating details and relationships in the score. Balanchine's choreography does this all the time. Yet it's just as musical, just as faithful to the music-dance marriage, when it asserts some independence. A little space between the music and dance opens up room to breathe. A little friction can make you hear more acutely.

Take what Balanchine does with the central Largo movement. The score is still a concerto for two violins, but one of the female soloists exits, replaced by a man. What follows is a duet, though it's a duet of a particular kind, since the central couple interacts as much with the female ensemble as they do with each other. It's predictable—and also beautiful and moving—that Bach's singing melody should be reflected by the man lifting the woman in high, sun-across-the-sky arcs. Yet, less predictably, he also lifts her over the ensemble dancers, who are grouped into two lines like hedgerows. Setting her down, he holds her hand high as she threads through them. When she and he entangle alone, the others sneak through the bridges of their limbs, multiplying boughs and branches, and eventually everyone, the man and all nine women, join hands in a giant daisy chain that winds and unwinds. This isn't what the two violins do, though of course it is.

Similarly, as the music repeats and the singing theme keeps returning, Balanchine doesn't just repeat. Near the end of the Largo, when the main theme returns for the final time, the second female soloist comes back, just for a moment—a freshening, suspense-building surprise before the man arcs the woman once again.

But there's still more going on in those lifts. The critic Edwin Denby, writing about *Concerto Barocco* when it was new, described the culmination of the lifts, when the woman slowly descends onto a single sharp point, as "a deliberate and powerful plunge into a wound." Balanchine often discounted this kind of talk as fancy. "A flower doesn't tell a story," he liked to say; "it itself is a beautiful thing." *Concerto Barocco* doesn't have characters; this isn't *Romeo and Juliet*. And yet Balanchine also said that two dancers on a stage "are already a story in themselves." He didn't need to add how much truer that is for two dancers with music. He knew that dance, because embodied, could never be wholly abstract, and neither, really, could music, which he said always leaves afterimages. He took those afterimages—our imaginations, pricked by the same music, all produce different ones—and he turned them into dance.

Denby's wound probably isn't Balanchine's afterimage; it isn't mine, and I can't always see it. But the remainder of Denby's sentence haunts me: "the emotion of it answers strangely to the musical stress." This gets at an aspect of the music-dance marriage that's hardest to discuss, especially relative to its large importance. As Denby noted, the moments he found "emotional" are "strictly formal as dance inventions." But those moments do answer strangely to the music—not analytically or even satisfyingly, but *strangely*—and when dance does that, it can take us deeper into the music than the music does alone.

This, I think, is the key to why *Concerto Barocco* and *Esplanade* can both be great. *Esplanade*, it should be said, isn't set only to that double concerto. Its first two sections come from Bach's Violin Concerto No. 2 in E Major. I suspect that Taylor made this choice so as to skirt the full force of the *Concerto Barocco* comparison, but the E Major Concerto suited his aim, too. An esplanade is a place you go to stroll, and the dance starts mainly with walking; a fanfare quality in the E Major Concerto ceremonializes this walking, even as the casual but structured ambling unstiffens the Bach. Also, I think that Taylor wanted two slow movements; the Adagio he takes from the E Major Concerto is a mournful one, which allows him to color walking with melancholy, giving an inward twist to circular treading. Here, dancers keep almost touching but never make contact. At the end of the movement, they crawl in a circle, haltingly, as if going down a drain.

That image answers strangely to the music, bringing out its quality of fateful winding down. And so do images that Taylor gives us during the double concerto's Largo. In truth, some of Taylor's version of the Largo seems shallower than Balanchine's. There are three male-female couples, and the suggested romance approaches Hallmark blithe. I find the dominant gesture—the men carrying the women in cradle position—sweet but a shade sexist and infantilizing. Still, some of the saccharin is cut by one's realization that these dancers are completing what their counterparts in the earlier Adagio could not. What Taylor hears—sequential imitations in threes, not just twos—never feels wrong, and there are moments that are strangely right. A woman puts her arms around a man's shoulders and swings out in circle after circle, perfectly answering the musical stress of one of Bach's climbing passages. Even better, when the singing theme returns for the final time, a man and woman roll over each other across the floor; then she steps on his stomach, steps down, climbs the hills of his supine form knee to hip, and stands on his stomach again. Now that's tenderness. Since Denby and Taylor were friends, I wonder if he was thinking of a woman's feet and her weight and wounds. In any case, the tone is Taylor's, the tenderness close to pain, and I'd swear it's in the Bach.

The Allegro finale is what I described before: the cascading waves of sliding, falling, running, leaping, and catching. This is joy, right? This is back to childhood. It's not even strange—once you've seen it—that it fits the music. Bach's Allegro is pell-mell. At the same time, though, because of what Taylor has already shown us, he brings out a desperation in the rhythmic propulsion. Dramatic gestures, twisting and spinning to the ground, return, faster now, but still trailing darkness. This shading is what's profound about Taylor's dance, and why it tallies with Bach. "The choreographer will never be able to achieve such precision in the expression of movement as a composer through sound effect," Balanchine wrote, always modest with respect to music. "Whenever I feel I have found the 'inevitable' moment, I can never be as sure as in music that it might not need some clarification after all." What *Concerto Barocco* and *Esplanade* show is that more than one moment can be inevitable, particularly when the music is infinite. This is the gift of the musical choreographer. Now, when I listen to the double concerto at home, the moments merge in my mind: the hopping on tiptoe as arms rise and fall like mad guillotines, the sliding and sliding and leaping and catching—all of it somehow in the Bach all along and now certainly in there forever, never again to be unseen, never to be unheard.

16 Edward Elgar: Cello Concerto in E Minor, 1919

PAUL MULDOON

1

Valiant old spear-man, old Elgar
of the high-gloss
finish, of the lacquer
smooth as glass

albeit derived from a coarse resin
itself derived from a tree-bug.
You'd long been able to refine
your experience against the Ninth Legion

into the ability to *roughen*
your style in that same region.
It stands to reason
a spear that's been at your beck

and call for ten centuries
of shield-walls
thrown up against all and sundry
might now resonate with the wails

of this one squaddy
picked at random from the orchestra,
with a rail-thin human body
in its death-throes.

2

Valiant old spear-man, old Elgar
of the mead-hall,
swapping that honey liquor
for a mud-hole

filled with urine
on the outskirts of Passchendaele.
You'd fritter and frolic
among daffodils and dandelions

and take time by the forelock
with the hunter, Orion.
It transpires his bow *is* backed with iron.
The bow-edge is dull

from the downward spiral
of forces once spryly mustered
that are now all splatter and sprawl.
The freshly-delivered mustard

gas is already
taking its toll on these tearful
boy-soldiers trying to hold steady
for the next interval.

3

Valiant old spear-man, old Elgar,
stalwart and staunch
against such forces as beleaguer
us here in the stench

of the dunghill
on which we've been thrown.
You'd been all but delirious
when you heard from across the Channel

the British and German artilleries
vie for a place in the annals.
It was somewhere there in the tangle
of duckboards and open drains

so many had struck a bargain
with history,
having once and for all broken
rank in a tumble of pale straw

and cadmium yellow.
Somewhere near Ypres
your own blood-burnished cello
must have fallen face-down in barbed wire.

17 Opera Is Indivisible

ALEXANDER KLUGE

A Power of Unearthly Origin

A small group of violence-prone Puritans from the Netherlands was conspiring. With relish. In protest. Iconoclasts and Anabaptists. The plan was to stir up the population of a German town while Mass was underway and strip the images from the walls of the cathedral. For the sake of the "pure word." With a racket. All superstition, all decoration, all *depictions* of the sacred, all the music, the choir—a clean sweep.

At the moment of peril—as told by Heinrich von Kleist—the notes of a salvific motet, composed more than a hundred years before by a Venetian master, were supposed to fill the church, placating the agitated townspeople and checking their destructive tendencies. But the nun who was to conduct the work was prostrated by fever, comatose. Thus Cecilia, that mother goddess of music, often confused with Diana, but also with Orpheus, son of Apollo, who in turn often took female form as Orphea or even as the lost Eurydice who after her death merged with her beloved, so filling him with his own yearning that the shift of sex from the singer Orpheus to the voice Orphea makes sense even to the strictest rationalist—that wise goddess of music stepped up to the conductor's stand (as the ghost of the fever victim) and by the seventh tap of the baton had conquered the crowd's lust for destruction.

The violence-prone characters from the Netherlands, lurking behind a church column, could not pull themselves together to carry out their plot.

Later these "thwarted" or "music-cleansed" men were found in a madhouse. Giving every appearance of contentment and a happy frame of mind, they spent years sitting at a table, croaking out snatches of sacred music, intonations, guttural sounds which experts identified as stemming from the legendary motet whose power had rescued the church. Heinrich von Kleist entitled his account of this incident, the briefest of his stories, "St. Cecilia, or THE POWER OF MUSIC."

Why Operas Do Not Make Concessions to the Ear

1

My father was the house doctor at the Halberstadt Municipal Theater. He didn't miss a single opera premiere. By profession he was also an obstetrician, and sometimes he'd be alerted to a birth while watching the opera. As a child, it was my task to act as messenger, bringing him the news and fetching him from the opera house. Stealing into that mysterious space and making my way to his seat in the second row, surrounded by sounds and bewildered by the onstage goings-on, my very first sensory impressions were of light and music. I understood nothing of those operas, but these glimpses were crucial: not only have I listened to opera all my life, I have sought to respond to the attraction of the opera in my literary works and films.

Children ought to be exposed to opera as early as possible, especially in its theatrical form, which brings together the context (the so-called plot) and the mysterious empire of hearing, the music, prompting an interplay between two different aspects of our brain and our senses.

Apollo, as we see in the finale of one of the very first operas, Monteverdi's *Orfeo*, is the father of Orpheus, the legendary musical enthusiast. Thus the god is the forefather of music—but also of premonitory intuition and mathematics. Fixated on our everyday reality (which does not always prove to be real) and on adult intelligence, which possesses a language of its own, we underestimate the legacy that each human being (and a child is, first and foremost, an "undistorted human being") carries on from evolution: skills in *mathematics* (which very few people really use, but which nonetheless is the language of the cosmos), the language of *music* (a form of intelligence that need not make sense, but is extremely diverse and orderly), and finally, *emotions* and *rationality*. Only the rare interplay of these abilities shows the full potential possessed by human beings, that is, children. Opera unites much of this potential (though sadly omitting mathematics). It benefits children to be introduced early to this Western achievement, and in the process opera can develop new forms. When opera is able to form fragments, to open up its chitin shell and offer a view of its details—in contrast to the classic hermetic canon—a contact surface emerges. That is what children need. They focus on the skin, not the whole.

Theodor W. Adorno, the greatest music lover among the philosophers, calls music a matter of trust. One must trust in its intimate force, that is, its rootedness in human beings, even those who do not believe in it. One must trust unwaveringly in the ears and the intelligence of children, who understand more than their teachers think. In other words, one should not adapt opera and music to children. Nor children to music. The encounter must be an unmediated one—it is then that the miracle occurs.

2

The first opera I ever attended was Puccini's *Tosca*. One day—the war was already on—my parents decided to send me to the Municipal Theater. That week, however, it was showing Gounod's *Margarethe*. No, said my father, we can't send the boy to see that, it's about abortion. But maybe he'll focus on the music, said my mother, and not notice the problematic parts? That's too risky, my father replied, who generally had a stricter mindset, though also a greater love of music; let's postpone the whole thing, he said, *Tosca* is playing soon. And so the first thing I saw was not the censored Faust opera, but the most dramatic of Italian operas, in which all the protagonists die at each other's hands in the course of a single day. Not exactly uplifting for a child's mind. Following their debut in my life, I have never stopped listening to operas; later on, in my work, I have tried to retell the history of opera using the techniques of film and literary narrative.

This kind of devotion arises not just through the music itself, but through observing other people's love of music, and in my case through my father's authority. Nor is it based on that one-time experience of *Tosca* (about which I have since created twenty stories and several film scenes), but above all on my father's habit of listening to opera on the radio every Sunday at 3 p.m. while writing up his invoices, a smorgasbord of *The Merry Wives of Windsor*, *Die Meistersinger von Nürnberg*, *Rigoletto*, but also *Wedding Night in Paradise*—a Berlin operetta—and the heavyweights *Carmen*, *Otello*, *Samson et Dalila*, erratic blocks surpassing my childish understanding, anchored in reality only by my father's authority.

Here we see that out in the world the love of opera, the love of music cannot emerge spontaneously or cannot express itself unless a crucial person or a public opera house is present to form a vessel in which the inclination develops. It takes serious places and persons to secure the child's wish. On the other hand, patronizing pedagogical concessions are not required. I did cry more readily at a well-composed, child-friendly opera such as Humperdinck's *Hansel and Gretel*. But that did not heighten my desire to "listen to more operas."

I believe that the seriousness operas can radiate—even so-called comic operas—imparts itself to a child's mind, creating an attraction unlike any of the attractions inherent in the new media. To sense this seriousness, it is not necessary to understand it. Children understand what death is without having it explained to them and without grasping the details. They have a direct, undistorted capacity for intuition, to which music and plot-based musical theater responds. Thus the relationship between children and opera should not be defined by compromises, but rather understood as a mutual challenge, a challenge that children are well able to handle.

3

Operas have been performed publicly for about the past 400 years. Xaver Holtzmann, author of the *Imaginary Opera Guide*, has counted a total of 80,000 operas, most of which are lost. If we were familiar with all of them, he says, taken together they would form one great score, a landscape of the human emotions brought forth by the modern age. Opera history, Holtzmann claims, is like a distorting mirror showing the peculiarities, errors, virtues and sins of bourgeois society and the industrial and digital societies that succeeded it, reflecting them like the faceted eye of the devil described in Andersen's fairy tale *The Snow Queen*.

When children encounter this musical repository of experiences, they have automatically found a "point beyond the earth," a point outside their everyday world that stimulates their imagination and self-awareness. It doesn't matter how much they "understand"; the important thing is that their unformed capacity for intuition is grappling with it: sensory flexibility emerges. The point is not what use this can be put to, the point is that it is a sensory enrichment, that it imparts the ability to experience moments of happiness.

It seems that humanity has survived the process of evolution only because it is able to orient itself in three extremely different spheres: in rationality, in religion, and in art. This triad, which no management consultant can possibly explain, is found in all forms of progress. When it comes to art, grown-up children test what is trustworthy mainly by ear. If I myself am asked to say honestly whether I trust more in language and images (my professional tools) or in music, I reply: in music, and in the music of language.

In his investigations, the Swiss educational researcher Piaget examined how children experience the world. For a long while, he says, children are active, learning and having different experiences, but understanding nothing. Suddenly, by leaps and ruptures, "understanding" coalesces within them like the crystal lattice in a chemical solution. They live and learn by leaps. And each of these surprising, lightning-like leaps includes elements of the previous stage.

This can be applied to children's encounter with the opera. Operas are generally written and composed for adults. Their sheer length challenges children's mental horizons. At the same time, I can offer no other solution: we must take the risk that children will understand operas on their own. It is more likely that challenges and misunderstandings will form the roots of a profound impression—an encounter such as those experienced by Adorno or Proust (or Mozart as a child)—than that music education or the persuasive powers of television will find the spot where a child's deep impressions are formed. Modern children sense when someone is trying to persuade them, and they know how to resist. In other words: no Sesame Street opera. Only the best, that is, the most complex opera is good enough for our children.

4

A number of operas concern children who are lost, or who suddenly reappear. In both cases, the effect can be explosive. Verdi's magnum opus *Simon Boccanegra*, which received a grand staging at the Staatsoper Unter den Linden with Plácido Domingo and Daniel Barenboim, centers on the long-lost daughter who turns out to be the granddaughter of Simon's most powerful rival. Her clear, high voice is unforgettable in the ensemble "Pace." *Rigoletto*, too, is about a father protecting his child. One is struck by the emotional force of the music that Verdi composed for the parting of the father, soldier, and musician Miller from his daughter Luisa, preceding Rigoletto's farewell from Gilda. These two related passages of the score could be played in succession to produce a contrast and a strong consonance. Wagner's Siegfried is another child hero, just as his protector and lover Brünnhilde is not just a powerful messenger of the gods and guarantor of the future, but also a loyal child. A touching aspect of Pfitzner's *Palestrina* is the observer who survives at the end: Palestrina's son. The series of emotional moments involving children suggests how important the continuation of the family was in older forms of society, that is, for all of our ancestors. It was not money that constituted true property, true wealth, but rather the people who married into the family, and the children resulting from the marriages. One is reminded that profound emotional responses are not based merely on current feelings; rather, these feelings evoke a wealth of potent overtones and echoes from the past. Judging by my observations, children are open to these impressions.

Even the Rosenkavalier and the very young woman he woos are more children than anything else. The antithesis to these happy children is seen in the harrowing scene in Alban Berg's *Wozzeck* in which Marie tells her children the tale of the moon. This segues back to the opera *Margarethe*, and the subject of infanticide, which culminates in Robert Schumann's "Chorus of the Unborn Children" in his setting of fragments of Act 5 of Goethe's *Faust*. But children under twelve would be banned from attending.

5

In the Age of Enlightenment, children were still being painted as miniature adults. The prince who would later be Frederick the Great is a knee-high officer standing next to the mighty leg of his authoritarian father, smoking a pipe in the company of his *Tabakskollegium*. Until the time of Classicism, this was the perspective of adult artists on children. They were steered to grow up—that is, to become real—as quickly as possible.

Our more nuanced attitude toward children in Central and Western Europe did not emerge until the second half of the bourgeois era. It is an achievement of modern society. In opera, a genre tending toward high art, the nuanced depiction of children's experience made little headway. The melodrama of the prince in Mozart's *Zaide* or the search for the pin in *Figaro* have more affinity with the world of children than do the children used as dramatic devices in the operas of the nineteenth and twentieth centuries. Operas, one could say in general, are a bit too grandly proportioned for children. One reason for this is that the rivalry among the great composers and librettists caused constant inflation in the genre. The tragic intensification of the finales of the third and fifth acts requires increasingly large, differentiated spheres of action, and finally the progression of the music calls for a trained ear.

In other words: where is music still naïve? Where can the high art of music, the opera, be entered with unsophisticated senses? A child does not yet have a budget of attention to last for three or more hours. If we are concerned with creating more proximity and contact surface between children and the world of opera, while refraining from damaging the rich, sensitive substance of opera through simplification and concessions to the ear, another option exists. We know that when it comes to ancient artworks, there is a great fondness for fragments. A fragment fascinates the imagination, which automatically fills in what is incomplete. Given the plethora of unknown operas, it is possible to present children with opera fragments without depriving opera history of its richness. I am not even remotely thinking of so-called greatest hits. Rather, subplots and lesser-known passages that make a self-contained impression are especially suited for children to focus on. First they must take possession of these "gems"; they can collect a whole string of such pieces. At the beginning of the third act of *Götterdämmerung,* Siegfried comes to the Rhine Maidens, who beseech him to throw the ring into the Rhine—this would end the curse and let the rest of the story unfold happily. For a reckless moment Siegfried is prepared to take off the ring and cast it away. But when the Rhine Maidens become too insistent, he refuses defiantly, and the catastrophe takes its course. Here Richard Wagner discovers new sounds, departing in many ways from the compositional norms he had followed before interrupting his work for so many years. And these sounds also differ from the fabric of music and leitmotifs that conclude the colossal piece. Rather than being immediately overwhelmed by the complete work, a young person would do better to start by exploring this self-contained scene, listening to it twelve to eighteen times played on the piano or conducted by different conductors, or in the same version, so as to become familiar with it. Indeed, all modern people, who must cope not only with art, but with media and realities that differ from those in the nineteenth, eighteenth, or sixteenth century, require such "lagoon beaches," that is, accessible perspectives on opera. When they move between the world of art and the outside world, people live amphibiously.

Here I am comparing reality, as presented in part in the internet's information masses (though what is real is not the mass of data, but the mass of facts outside), with an ocean, and the world of art as the solid ground on which we (like our ancestors) occasionally crawl.

6

True opera constitutes a counterworld. For that reason, it need have no fear of manifesting itself in different forms in this world (for instance, in the new media), staking out its "hallowed garden" there—its *hortus conclusus*. In this sense one could regard opera itself as a child. It had a happy phase when it was invented, in the "musical dramas" of Jacopo Peri, Claudio Monteverdi, and Francesco Cavalli. Later on, it recovered from paralysis over and over again, taking new turns and laying claim to a new simplicity. One of the theaters where Giuseppe Verdi's works premiered, La Fenice (which burned down thrice and was rebuilt each time), harks back to the legendary bird Phoenix, which goes up in flames but is always reborn. That could be the emblem of opera, whose concentration of artistic forms means that its expressive diversity is matched by no other genre.

I have been struck by the special affinity between modern forms of opera and early forms from the seventeenth century. Both, it seems, are still young. If film montage directly confronts a fragment of Monteverdi's music with a fragment by Rihm, Lachenmann, or Bernd Alois Zimmermann, the effect is that of timelessness. The fragments fit together as though there were no intervening centuries.

Another example: as the canon of the *opera seria* aged (it could depict nothing but gods, heroes, and authority figures), a young form of opera developed in the breaks between the acts, for instance Pergolesi's *La serva padrona*, operas no more than twenty minutes in length in which musical voice was lent to everyday life, comedy, real people. Out of this youthful form, tempestuous Italian opera developed, leading to Bellini, Donizetti, and Verdi. Here we recognize two fundamental laws of evolution: it always favors small organisms; and long childhoods, for instance in elephants and human beings, ensure differentiation in adulthood. This is too positively phrased to apply to entire societies, but it holds for the history of opera.

What would it mean to see opera itself as a child in the twenty-first century? I can't imagine that it will ever return to being a major form sustained by an intact, self-confident bourgeois public, as in the pre-1914 era. If it focused on that alone, it would become nothing but repertory.

While preparing his production of *Tristan* in Bayreuth, Heiner Müller flew over Siberia to Japan, where a conference on the future of opera in the twenty-first century was being held. He prepared for his brief talk at the conference by filling out notecards, and meanwhile a quarter of the earth's surface passed below him, visible through the airplane window. This gave rise to Müller's idea of the anti-opera. It is like partisans confronting a battalion in official parade formation: scattered throughout the terrain in concealment, outwardly unprepossessing, highly motivated and bellicose. None of these characteristics could be ascribed to the parading troops in their traditional uniforms, clearing their throats as they fall into formation, said Müller. What would be the function of an anti-opera in the twenty-first century? Müller's reply: It would be a message in a bottle. It would be news of utopia, of human potential.

On the very same day as I worked on this essay, I honored Müller—who is not dead as long as he has friends to perpetuate his ideas—by creating together with my staff a film fragment which we shall regard as a very small opera organism. The music, performed on the piano, is by Franz Schubert. In the song "Wie Ulfru fischt," the young trout (children of the brook) sing: "The earth has tremendous beauty, but safety it has none."

Adorno once told me that this rather short song was one of his favorite pieces of music. The film shows no water and no fisherman, but a concrete German fortress built in 1898 near Metz. The strikingly "modern" fortress structures formed the prototype of what would later be the Maginot Line, in which France placed its hope and trust in 1940. Here the substance of the opera (namely, the faith that such fortresses—tremendous and in a sense even beautiful—provide safety) is contained in the actual circumstances, and is no doubt lost to modern memory. At the same time we hear Schubert's melodrama, the song of the fish in the water, a metaphor for the partisans. Several minutes long, the film is assembled from the vocabulary of moving images, from YouTube and from old music, and hints at what Heiner Müller pictured in Japan or during a break from working on his production in Bayreuth when he thought about opera in the twenty-first century. The subject was a new one for him, a mature writer who discovered his passionate interest in opera only toward the end of his life. As he put it:

> When all has been said, the voices turn
> Sweet; then comes opera.

"When all has been said"—that is one of the elegiac exaggerations to which Heiner Müller was prone. We are not living at the end of days. There is an incredible amount yet to be told, sorted, and composed. The arts are facing such challenges that they must leave the solid structures of high art. Müller's actual behavior contradicts his skeptical thinking: the year he died, he was planning for the Berliner Ensemble theater a musical drama on the subject of the financial crisis (it had not even come into existence, and already Müller was responding to it), based on Dirk Baecker's book *Postheroisches Management* (*Post-heroic Management*). In such a context voices turn emphatic, not sweet. The child called opera has yet to complete its education.

An Acrobat of the Body, the Ear, and Her Head's Two Cooperating Hemispheres

The *Goldberg Variations*. Never was a sack of gold coins invested better than by the tsar's envoy at the Saxon court, Count Keyserlingk, who could not sleep at night and commissioned these variations from Bach. The pianist Simone Dinnerstein has flown in from

New York. She approaches the material in a new way. She shovels the sound masses against one another, respecting their imbalances. Asymmetry rather than a schema. The masses of notes do not follow any beat, producing arrhythmias as if choirs positioned in different wings of old churches were responding to one another, but the church spaces were distorting the arrival of the notes at one's ears. That is in keeping with Bach, who did not obey the metronome but, rather, the immanent gravity of the note sequences, as had been customary in the late Middle Ages. For her version, the pianist has radically altered the distribution of the rhythmic and melodic arches between the left and right hands (and the fingerings). The left and right hands cross and follow each other with great élan, each seamlessly continuing the other's movement. It is difficult to assess what that means for the left and right hemispheres of the brain, which govern the right and left hands respectively. An acrobat of the body, the ear, and her head's two cooperating hemispheres.

An exchange with Dan Diner that same evening. The historian received a major European award accompanied by research funds. He is interested in portraying German-French relations between 1931 and 1945 (that is approximately the duration of the Second World War in his view, if one includes the Japanese invasion of Manchuria). He analyzes the "Persian Corridor," which is barely known. Via railway tracks and roads running through a British zone and a Soviet zone that divided Iran, the Allies sent supplies to Russia during the war. And one mustn't view Stalingrad in the West-East direction, Dan Diner states, but in terms of its north-south supply route. Stalingrad kept this Persian Corridor open. It was on this Iranian terrain that the Cold War later began. In 1945 the Russians refused to vacate their zone. Later on, the British-Indian troops in that corridor would in turn topple Prime Minister Mosaddegh, thus making political processes in Persia irreversible. I feel slightly embarrassed about the brief section in the "history of a single day." On the other hand, Dan Diner encourages me. Hardly anyone knows about the Persian Corridor. But it marks a historical trail leading to the most dangerous Middle Eastern conflicts of today, and extends back far beyond 1921 (Lord Curzon). Here political reality worked on writing its own "narrative," unnoticed by the central power of historiography or public attention.

18 Music as a Family Affair

RUTH BADER GINSBURG AND JAMES GINSBURG

Interviewed by Nina Totenberg; chronicled by Melissa Lane

Organized by Marna Seltzer; recorded by Henry Valoris; transcribed by Lisa Tkalych

Music—as a matter of education, practice, absorption, and delight—is a vein that runs through and unites the Ginsburg family. In speaking together with Nina Totenberg about their shared and separate musical journeys, Justice Ginsburg and her son, James Ginsburg, described the way that they discovered music—both as a world in general, and in terms of individual works, performers, recordings, and stagings—and the role played by educators and family members in opening the doors of that world to them. This piece is an impression from that conversation, which I was privileged to listen in on, in the Lawyers' Lounge of the Supreme Court on May 16, 2018. Justice Ginsburg recalled her own introduction to music as vividly as she recalled moments of opening that door in turn for James and, earlier, for her daughter, Jane. James, in turn, was led through music to his distinguished career as a producer and to his marriage to a singer. Their shared bond with Nina Totenberg has likewise grown out of music and family as much as the law, going back to the relationship with Totenberg's father, the renowned violinist Roman Totenberg.

Justice Ginsburg first discovered classical music through the pianist Isidor Gorn, who was involved in the annual Gilbert and Sullivan production at her summer camp, and who taught her piano lessons during the school year in a soundproof studio on West 73rd Street. Kiki, the nickname by which Justice Ginsburg was known to her family and childhood friends, began taking piano lessons at the age of eight. Later, she also took up the cello, "because," she said, "you can get a decent tone from a cello a lot earlier than you could with a violin."

NT: Were you any good?

RBG: No. But I spent a lot of time. There was a period when I would practice up to three hours a day.

NT: And you still weren't any good? So, you know, for a lot of eight-year-old children that's a torture that you have to practice and then have to play this music. And you're not particularly good at it. What enchanted you at that age?

RBG: The music. And when I was in high school, I took up the cello so I could be in the school orchestra. That was a wonderful experience . . .

NT: Of course the cello was almost as big as you were. Did you store it at school?

RBG: No, I was using the school cello. Then I purchased my own, and we had three rows of cellists. I was always in the very last seat for cellos. I had no ambition to move up. I just wanted to be in the orchestra.

That level of clarity and self-knowledge as a child—choosing to practice for sheer love of doing so, choosing to learn an instrument in order to be able to harmonize with others, understanding that one need not excel in every pursuit in order to gain true and lasting value from it—was perhaps an early indication of the unusual person the future Justice would become.

Justice Ginsburg then described how she imbued her children with a love of music.

RBG: When Jane was four years old, I took her to the Amato Opera in New York. They do abbreviated operas, and they were doing *Trovatore*. After about ten minutes or so, Jane stood up and screamed at the top of her lungs. That's what it sounded like to her. I decided it was a little premature. Then we waited until she was eight, and we took her to *Così fan tutte* at the Met. We sat in the Family Circle in the very first row so she didn't have heads to look over. I bought her patent leather shoes and a velvet jumper, with a blouse to match.

It was a very special occasion. We also had a libretto with us. This *Così* was sung in English. So by the time we went to the opera, Jane knew most of the words and she loved it.

When she began to take her lively and rambunctious son, James, to concerts, it was easy to interest him, even at age five (a minor revelation of the interview was Justice Ginsburg's mention of this age, to which James said he "never knew"). As the Justice recalled: "If I took him to the Little Orchestra Society Concerts at Hunter College, he was rapt attention. He wasn't squirming and fidgeting. And when he was older he graduated to the Philharmonic," namely, to Michael Tilson Thomas conducting the Young People's Concerts.

Almost as soon as his mother had opened the doors to music, James set off on his own distinctive path of discovery that was focused as much on recordings as on attending live concerts: "I started collecting recordings when I was, I think, six or seven." Using his allowance to buy records of his own, he also listened avidly to his parents' collection, "the Toscanini Beethoven recordings and whatnot."

JG: I became a pretty serious collector. In fact, there is a funny story from my high school, which was Georgetown Day School here in Washington: my English teacher also worked part-time at what used to be called Olsson's Records here. He made the mistake one day of telling me that he would be glad to use his employee discount on my behalf. So every Monday I would trot into the faculty room for that stack of records that I had him buy me.

The devotion to collecting led to a "formative" summer job at Nonesuch Records; running the classical format and serving as the classical music DJ for the campus radio station as an undergraduate at the University of Chicago (WHPK); and eventually, to reviewing recordings for American Record Guide. "In the process," James said, "I started to notice quite a difference in the quality of production from one recording to another and began to realize that the producer makes a big difference, sometimes even more than who the artists are."

Despite this insight, and even after several years working in music PR after college, James still considered his eventual vocation to be the career in law that his parents and sister had likewise chosen. But already during the summer before starting law school at the University of Chicago, he realized that Chicago had even more to offer in a wealth of remarkable musicians who were nevertheless going largely unrecorded.

JG: One thing I had noticed about Chicago was that there were all these wonderful artists I would hear in concerts and live performances on the radio, and then I would go to record stores to look for their recordings, and there were none. (This was back when there were record stores.) The only recording activity going on in Chicago in the late '80s for classical music was the Chicago Symphony under Georg Solti. All these wonderful artists were being overlooked, because the major and even the independent labels were all based either in New York or on the West Coast. So I had the idea that I could start recording some of these people. And I began with a wonderful Russian émigré pianist whom I knew from his piano performances in Chicago. I even had taken some lessons from him. Then I recorded a composer-pianist at the University of Chicago, and then a harpsichordist-organist who played all over town, but again, you couldn't find him on any recordings. Very quickly this started to take on a life of its own. I actually produced the first recording over the summer before starting law school, so it came out just as I was starting law school.

The die was cast: James discovered pretty quickly that he liked producing recordings a lot more than he liked going to law school. Artists began to flock to the newly established label, Cedille Records, drawn by the reputation of the quality of the work being done by James Ginsburg as producer and by his engineer, to the point that James dropped out of law school in his second year to devote himself full time to the label. Soon he chose to turn the label into a nonprofit, so as to be able to raise money to record well beyond the initial focus (for reasons of economy) on solo keyboard. The catalogue now spans "the whole gamut from soloists to chamber groups to symphonies to choruses to opera recordings," and was described by Totenberg in connoisseurial terms as "the stuff of an almost bygone era" in light of the attentiveness shown by James and his team to the details of the performances and recordings.

Nina and James bantered during their conversation about a recording by her father, which she once found as a little girl in his studio, of a Mozart violin concerto with soloist André Gabriel. As Nina recalled: "I had never heard of André Gabriel, and I knew most of the violinists of that era. So I said to him, 'Who is André Gabriel?' And he said, 'Oh, that's me. I was under contract to Columbia. I couldn't record under my own name [on another label] and I needed some more money, so I became André Gabriel.'" To which James, the professional record producer, replied deadpan: "We've never done that."

The conversation finally turned back to Justice Ginsburg's own childhood, to explore one of the best-known facts about her musical identity: her passion for opera. Where did it begin?

RBG: I was introduced to opera at age eleven by a wonderful man. My aunt, who was a high school English teacher, took me to Brooklyn High School for a performance of *La Gioconda*. It was abbreviated into one hour. There was bare staging, but there were costumes. And the director narrated in between. I was just overwhelmed by it: the music and the story. I had not seen anything like opera. So that's when it started. . . .

The man who was putting on those operas for children was named Dean Dixon. As his career demonstrated, music in those days (as today) was not immune to the injustices of the wider society. Justice Ginsburg recalled that Dixon, who was African American, left the United States for Europe in the late 1940s, after having devoted himself to conducting an all-city children's orchestra and to other activities that introduced children to music in New York City for years; nevertheless, as he said then, "No one has ever called me Maestro." It took some twenty years for him to return permanently to the United States, and at least by then some things had changed: a measure of the change in American society in those twenty years is that in the late 1960s "every major orchestra in the country wanted him as a guest conductor"—and, finally, as "Maestro."

Mother and son then reflected on pieces of music that had particularly moved them. For the Justice, as a piano student, it was Chopin's Nocturnes and Preludes; then, in college, listening to the

Toscanini recording of *La Traviata*; and, eventually, discovering the unique marriage of music and words in the three operas composed by Mozart to libretti by Da Ponte. Whereas Ruth Bader Ginsburg was born a New Yorker, Da Ponte had become one. He was born a Jew in Italy, became a Catholic priest with a taste for the good life, and eventually fled his creditors to become the first professor of Italian at Columbia University. Of the three operas that he and Mozart produced in collaboration, in Justice Ginsburg's opinion the libretto of *Così* is slightly less good, but it is impossible for her—despite her decisiveness on the bench—to choose between the libretti of *The Marriage of Figaro* and *Don Giovanni*. In the conversation, however, it emerged that the latter has at least one edge in her experience as a music lover:

RBG: The Don that I heard most often was Cesare Siepi. And you could understand why any woman would be overwhelmed by him. He was a wonderful singer and a *very handsome* man. Every time I go to the *Don* and someone else is singing, I remember Cesare Siepi . . . he was the ultimate Don. . . . The sexiest duet in all of opera is between Zerlina and the Don. It is "Là ci darem la mano."

James Ginsburg's own answer to the question of pieces that matter to him turned back again to music that he discovered for himself growing up—especially just after they had moved to Washington, DC, when his mother ascended to the Supreme Court. The National Symphony gave a concert as a seventy-fifth birthday tribute to the Russian composer Dmitri Shostakovich, conducted by the composer's son Maxim, with Rostropovich (the music director) playing the First Cello Concerto, performed alongside the Second Piano Concerto and the Sixth Symphony. According to James, "There was just something about this music that was so new to me, and there was just such raw emotion in it. I immediately went to the Martin Luther King Library [their local neighborhood library in DC] and started pulling all their Shostakovich recordings"—the string quartets, the old Borodin Quartet recordings, the symphony recordings—"and very quickly this became my favorite composer."

When he first discovered Shostakovich, he knew nothing about the history and the struggles behind the music: "It was just the music itself that captured me." But as in the case of Dean Dixon, Shostakovich's career in music was subject to the injustice and oppression of the wider society, and in James's experience, "You can't not think about that once you've learned the history." As he came to realize, "This is a composer who somehow managed to capture in music all the suffering of the Russian people under Stalin and the other Soviet dictators, and you hear that particularly in pieces like the Tenth Symphony, written right after Stalin died, and the First Violin Concerto, written right before Stalin died."

Both Ginsburgs have continued to make musical discoveries for themselves over the years, finding new favorites in the modern repertoire in particular. For Justice Ginsburg, these include *Billy Budd* by Benjamin Britten; *The Rake's Progress* by Igor Stravinsky; *Cold Mountain* by Jennifer Higdon; and *Dead Man Walking* and *Moby-Dick* by Jake Heggie. In fact, the Justice keeps a page of the score of *Moby-Dick* signed by the composer in her chambers, a keepsake that accords with her interest in modern art more broadly: among the artworks that she has chosen from the collection of the Smithsonian (a prerogative accorded to every Justice) are two early Rothkos and two works by Josef Albers.

For James Ginsburg, music is now vocation, his life's work. For his mother, it is avocation, but it can be all-absorbing when she allows herself to enter it. This is usually, of course, as an audience member, taking a brief break from her legal duties: "I'm always thinking about the cases and how they should come out, and if I'm writing an opinion, how I should write it. But if I go to a good opera, I don't think about the law at all. I just enjoy the performance." Yet even better than being in the audience of an opera is being in the cast—albeit in a nonspeaking or a speaking-only role (for, as the Justice remarked wistfully, "I wish I could sing"):

RBG: The first time I had that experience [of appearing onstage in an opera], I was a super in *Fledermaus*. And for the guests at the ball onstage, the guest entertainer was Plácido Domingo. I was sitting very close to him, and it was like an electric current running through me.

Of course, she is never uncritical, even of her beloved Mozart and Da Ponte. Take for example the dubious gender politics in *Così*:

RBG: That whole idea that a woman who is in love and is engaged can be swept off her feet within twenty-four hours.

NT: That wasn't true for you—or was it true for you?

JG (speaking for his mother): Only by Cesare Siepi.

19 Your Brother Called

SUSAN WHEELER

Let us go on for a moment to something else found in the dossier...

ROBERT ASHLEY, *eL/Aficionado*

The secret agency of your recognitions after so many
years can drive the car all the long   uphill drive

way you will notice you noticed you may   in the split of
the café curtains   perfect for entertaining

a boy although he will he has   may surprise you with
all he keeps to himself   seeds of dissing of maligning

of injuries the pings and carrion the herbivores   by keeping
to himself he can water them   the car comes to a soft stop its

engine off only peepers now   the woods on either side of the house
spitting fireflies   the reference to India earlier red

and yellow in the camera in your head   that's enough
of that banality the boy is holding the packet

of oyster crackers over his soup and he will not look at
you when you enter   the phone ringing and he studiously

begins to pour   SWM athletic cultured   likes
hockey   weekend walks in simooms   don't forget

to swipe to cease the ring   multilingual theater loving
non-smoking seeks   it is as though the boy hasn't

heard will not hear may not   the telephone telephone was
there a mere boy he begins to eat the soup   it is

tomato soup and you are distracted by his incisors they
are small like he is small   his small incisors on the

crackers until sodden clump on his tongue and still   what
was the light like then   he does not look at you

in your twenties twenty six seven one spring
you cut the key the motor the Econoline a rest stop on

Taconic woods before the van   a silence suddenly
an old Saab beside you two dogs circling its seats their manes

one brass one a smear of cheese on dark rye the fulness   you
don't know how to say this   the feeling was a strange one

of bounty of overflow   the light of late sun now on gray sky
drops still shaking the pane beside you and the window the dogs

fill and you   the replete a finch flown suddenly and gone
can I bring you back to what is at hand sir the boy the oncoming

stars your resignation   I would say he was four feet five
but he sat in a leather chair higher than you would expect

the boy at a regular kitchen table eating his soup   you said
he is you say he was   you   he is the kind of

strawberry blond that time reddens maybe four feet six
your brother calls   DWT cultured well-travelled seeks

the gorged seedlings   the artillery of his privacy   boy
inking was inking the negatives   not seedlings but ivies

and the parasitic vine of cuscuta   back in the apartment
waiting for the call the shouting returns in the audio recorder

in your head   the dodder   the boy stands on the leather seat
of his chair   ***BROTHER YOU HAVE WRONGED SMOTE***

INJURED ME   outcome   his incisors in the crackers the sudden
sharp of a starling angry at your car   parked car in the drive

way you drive you drove it later without   the boy standing
on the leather seat over the tabletop green placemats

spit of soup hardening like acid tabs a sugar H peeled for a
birthday cake   your brother calls   the shouting means

you cannot hear him   when did the strangers take over
the bodies you once knew like you knew your own   hang

up   detach the lens   lay your shell down   the lamp is on
in the dark room   it is a word we use in the bureau

the boy's father   MWBM   the boy seeks
mightily armed and mightily armored perfect for entertaining

studio with sleeping loft call   terrarium boy shouted
from the tangle of his vines   we have

your observations what you will describe what you have
most of what happened is covered the boy and his dodder armor

binding the soft place in the mere skull the shouting of the boy

20 Holy Song of Thanks

ELAINE PAGELS

On an early summer afternoon in Colorado, my husband and I hiked up a dirt trail into the mountains for two and a half hours, trekked through pine forests, and scrambled through a boulder field before reaching Buckskin Pass, where, at over 11,000 feet, tiny blue wildflowers blossomed among traces of snow. Later, heading back down toward town, we walked into the music tent just as members of the Juilliard String Quartet were tuning their instruments. Then, as the chatter of thousands of people hushed to hear them, they began to play the opening chords of Beethoven's String Quartet in A Minor, Op. 132.

I'd never heard music more clear, intense, and powerful than we heard it that afternoon. Years later, when I asked Robert Mann whether he could remember playing that quartet on that particular summer day in Colorado, he instantly nodded, and said *yes*: that on that day, when playing the astonishing third movement that Beethoven called a "holy song of thanks to God for healing in time of illness," he himself had just recovered from an injury to his bowing arm—and felt as though he were dancing the music. Beethoven alternates two very different kinds of music in that movement: it opens with a four-note motif, played *molto adagio*, slow and sustained, solemnly imitated by each instrument in turn and leading to a mysteriously austere hymnlike texture; then, after a pause, the music crescendos, breaking into a brighter key and quicker tempo, stepping forth with a confident rhythm, trilling violin, and deftly spun melodic elaborations, all resonating with the quickened sense of recovery after illness. Beethoven himself marked this latter music with the words "Feeling new strength."

After that concert, unexpectedly, we came to know Robert Mann—Bobby, as everyone called him—and his wife Lucy, their daughter Lisa, and son Nicholas. We'd come to Aspen that summer for the Aspen Institute of Physics, where my husband engaged in research with other scientists, and they'd come for the Music Festival. Bobby was in the same seminar on Chinese and Indian culture in which I'd been invited to participate, and he and my husband struck up a friendship, having discovered a shared love of music and hiking in the mountains.

The music that first stopped me in my tracks, one day when I was seven years old—mesmerized, listening with my whole being—was a recording of Beethoven's Seventh Symphony. That felt different from the austere Beethoven, who was one of the piano gods in our home, where the piano held a place of honor, upon which a bust of Beethoven scowled from a perch above the keyboard, and those of Bach and Mozart presided on left and right. As a young child, I'd often heard my mother playing music, usually returning to Chopin, her favorite. During the piano lessons required of my brother and me, as well as all of our cousins, I'd labored over simplified versions of Bach's Gavotte, Beethoven's *Für Elise*, and Mozart's waltz from *Don Giovanni*. Later, in junior high and high school, I fell in love with a wide spectrum of other music—dancing to Elvis, Fats Domino, Louis Armstrong playing W. C. Handy's blues, the Beatles, Aretha Franklin. Yet through all those years, Beethoven's music wove the prominent theme.

After that first experience of hearing the Juilliard Quartet and meeting the Mann family, I loved seeing the closeness that they shared; how Lucy, who often performed with her husband, and her daughter Lisa, a dancer, shared so much, confiding in each other; and how their son Nicholas, undaunted by his father's fame, went on to blossom as an outstanding violinist, playing sparkling duets with his father, and later going on to his own musical career, forming his own quartet and performing throughout the world. We were also astonished to learn that we were already neighbors in New York. For when we all returned there in the fall, where Heinz was doing physics at Rockefeller University, and I was starting to teach at Barnard and Columbia, Bobby was the star violinist teaching at Juilliard; and he and his family lived in an apartment on Central Park West, half a block from our apartment, a fourth-floor brownstone walkup on West 87th Street.

As neighbors, we shared much of family life, including, of course, the joy of our son Mark's birth, the somber shadow of his diagnosis of pulmonary hypertension, and the unutterable grief of his death, when he was six years old. When Bobby heard of this, he generously offered to come with other musicians to the service at the Church of the Heavenly Rest, where they played a movement of exquisite music—the echo in my memory recalls it as the Adagio from the Schubert Quintet.

The following December, my husband and I sat close together on the floor at the Manns' Christmas party, hearing the musicians play again the Beethoven quartet Op. 132, with its remarkable central movement. As before, we could hear how this astonishing movement sustains and explores contrasting tempos and tones, at moments moving through hymnic chords, somber and deep, then opening into a higher register and a faster pace, those slower tones suddenly "feeling new strength." This time when hearing the "song of thanks to God" break into a joyful cascade of music, I vividly envisioned our son Mark exuberantly pedaling his small red bicycle on a path through Central Park, as I jogged along beside him, as so often we'd done during his lifetime.

Shortly after that, realizing that now we needed children to love as much as any children might need parents, we adopted two babies from the Edna Gladney Center in Fort Worth, Texas: a daughter, Sarah, and an infant son, whom we named David. Yet during the following summer in Colorado, our small family was shattered by another, entirely sudden shock, when Heinz, having gone out for his usual Saturday hike in the mountains, slipped as a rock on his path broke, and fell to his death from Pyramid Peak. Again, our friends came through, Bobby bringing a quartet to the service, this time at Rockefeller University; I was especially grateful for their presence, although of that day only flashes of memory remain.

During the interminable months that followed, dark beyond imagining, and mainly lost, like distant galaxies, in black holes in space, I could hardly bear to listen to any music. When members of the quartet invited me to Alice Tully Hall at Lincoln Center to hear Schoenberg's music, I listened as long as I could, then suddenly got up and rushed out of the concert hall, feeling that the dissonances were tearing me apart. I ran down the New York streets toward Central Park West to the Lutheran church near 66th Street, where I knew that the choir would be singing a Bach cantata that afternoon, as they did every Sunday during the church year. I slipped into a wooden seat at the back of the church, where the clear architectonic structure of Bach's music offered what felt like relief. There, instead of bracing myself against sound that came at me like a challenge, I was grateful for Bach's calm, deliberate pacing of the organ's introductory sounds. As the choir joined in, feeling welcomed into the deep warmth of their harmonies, I began to sit straighter, breathe more deeply, and find some equanimity, as evening darkened into night.

After that, whenever I had to travel between New York, where we still lived, and Princeton, where I went to work, I carried a Walkman with CDs and headphones, hoping to shield myself from outside noise. At that time, nearly the only music I could bear to hear was that of Beethoven's late quartets, to which I listened, obsessively, for months and years thereafter. In these late works, Beethoven allows contrasts to emerge and remain unreconciled, with the result that he articulates experiences much deeper and more complex than anything but his music could express. Nothing else, and surely nothing less, than the heights they scaled and the depths they plumbed could serve as solace during such a time.

Now that many decades have passed since then, life renewing itself has restored a much wider range of music to me, from Ray Charles to Mozart's *Magic Flute* to the Grateful Dead, and many other joys as well. But having experienced music's healing power, I still find none more poignant and powerful than Beethoven's quartet Op. 132 and its holy song of thanks.

21 On Beethoven's String Quartet in B-flat, Op. 130, with the *Grosse Fuge*

ARNOLD STEINHARDT

Interviewed by Scott Burnham

Musicologist Scott Burnham interviewed Arnold Steinhardt, first violinist of the Guarneri String Quartet, in Steinhardt's New York City apartment, on February 21, 2018. The topic was Beethoven's late string quartet in B-flat, Op. 130. Beethoven composed Op. 130 in 1825–26. It was premiered in Vienna by the Schuppanzigh Quartet on March 21, 1826. The original version consists of six movements: Adagio ma non troppo–Allegro; Presto; Andante con moto ma non troppo; Alla danza tedesca (Allegro assai); Cavatina (Adagio molto espressivo); Grosse Fuge. At the behest of his publisher, Beethoven later composed an alternative finale (Allegro).

SB: You obviously have a lot of history with Op. 130 and the *Grosse Fuge*. If I have it right, you read through it for the first time almost sixty years ago, in 1959, at Curtis. And you recorded it for the first time in the late '60s, about fifty years ago. Then you recorded it again about thirty years ago, in the late '80s. And you performed it in concerts with the Guarneri Quartet for over forty years, sometimes as part of a Beethoven cycle.

AS: Yes, and sometimes by itself, and sometimes with the Great Fugue, and sometimes with the second finale. I would imagine without exaggeration that we've performed Op. 130 well over one hundred times.

SB: So what was your first encounter with this quartet like?

AS: I came upon it not just as a student but as a student who was innocent in terms of chamber music and string quartets. I had a rather insulated but maybe typical musical beginning, in that, like so many of my friends, I wanted to be the next flaming soloist. So I studied all the pieces that one studies to become the next virtuoso. And my teachers *never* talked about string quartets or chamber music; it was Paganini and more elevated things, even the Beethoven Violin Concerto. I had a teacher when I was growing up in Los Angeles, the great virtuoso Toscha Seidel, who trotted me through all of the violin repertoire, and only years later did I discover that he played string quartets every Friday night with his cronies for fun. In those days, chamber music, by and large, was for fun, certainly in America. But to make a living from it? "No, no, no, you can't do that."

So I came to the Curtis Institute of Music as a seventeen-year-old, never having studied a string quartet, knowing almost nothing about chamber music, and I was rather annoyed when I was required to study a Mozart string quartet with Jascha Brodsky (the first violinist of the venerable Curtis String Quartet). Because I thought, "What is this? It's so hard to fit in. You have to play with other people. You have to be together with other people. This is uncomfortable. It's beautiful music, but it's too difficult. You're in a straitjacket."

And then a violinist who had graduated from the Curtis Institute of Music, Henri Temianka (I knew him because he lived in Los Angeles), formed a very successful string quartet, the Paganini String Quartet. Maybe as a kind of thank you to Curtis for having put him up, he came with his quartet and played a concert for us. This was a year or two before four of us decided to get together and study Op. 130 with the Great Fugue. Their concert was an eye opener and an ear opener for me, because they performed Op. 132, the quartet Beethoven composed right before Op. 130, one of the three quartets commissioned by Prince Galitzin. Op. 132 contains the slow movement in which Beethoven gives thanks to the deity for convalescing after a serious illness, and it lasted forever. I thought I had gone into some kind of space travel. I had never heard anything like that or felt anything like that before. The classical music repertoire is exalted, and there are all kinds of emotional peaks in it that I was somewhat acquainted with already as a seventeen- or eighteen- or nineteen-year-old, but this was something entirely different. I became curious about Beethoven's string quartets at that point, and I had the feeling that if one quartet went to Mars, another went to Venus, and a third went to Uranus—it was space travel. So when my friend John Dalley, who became the second violinist in the Guarneri Quartet, approached me and said he thought it would be a nice idea to get together and study this late Beethoven quartet, Op. 130, with the *Grosse Fuge*, I said, "What is the *Grosse Fuge*?" And he said, "Well, it's the Great Fugue; it's this crazy and wonderful piece, and would you want to be in the group as second violinist?" and I said, "Well, yeah." So the four of us studied it all year long, and then we performed it in Curtis Hall. This was such a magnificent experience for me that I looked up at everybody in the middle of the slow dreamy section of the Great Fugue and I thought, "Oh, to be playing this kind of music with these people. What a privilege!" And then I looked down at the music and realized I was lost, in the first performance I ever gave of this piece. I was so embarrassed! It felt like it lasted forever, when it might have been five or ten seconds.

I didn't realize it at the time, but this was the beginning of a turning point in my life. I still wanted to be a soloist, and I was still entering competitions and performing with orchestras. But the experience of playing quartets remained with me when I left school, and I kept on thinking, I'm doing this for fun, when, in effect, I was gradually reordering my professional life until I finally realized that it would be a dream to be able to play this kind of music for the rest of my life.

But you know it's also interesting that there is this select group of composers who spent their whole lives writing string quartets. Not every one of the great composers, but Haydn and Mozart and Beethoven and Schubert and Mendelssohn. And Dvořák and Bartók and Shostakovich. They were some of the ones who composed quartets their whole lives, and there are a lot of other composers who didn't even bother writing one. And people like Ravel and Debussy who thought, "Well, I'm not a composer unless I write at least one string quartet," and what great string quartets they were, but they went on to other things. Beethoven, though—he realized that the string quartet was his ticket to a different kind of creativity.

SB: It makes sense to think so, because his string quartets extend along the whole course of his mature career. And they were what he ended with.

AS: I always think of something Einstein was quoted as saying: that everything should be as simple as possible but no simpler. To me that's the essence of the string quartet, and that's one of the things that attracted me as a young musician to the string quartet: nothing extraneous, just the absolute core of simplicity. But when you reduce it down to three instruments (and there are some great pieces written for string trio), you find composers adding double stops to the music so that it winds up in effect being like a quartet, a poor man's quartet.

SB: So what do you make of Beethoven's Op. 130 when it is played with the *Grosse Fuge* as its finale?

AS: I am reminded of Elisabeth Kübler-Ross's book on death and dying and all the stages of grief. After four movements that are alternately magnificent and modest, with no sense of them being connected in any apparent way, a door suddenly opens into a church where a soulful hymn is heard [Ed: the Cavatina movement]. And then one of the most remarkable things in music happens: in the middle of this hymn, a human being loses his way. The movement lapses into a very unexpected key during this desperate strait, and Beethoven creates the lost soul with the first violin's line, because almost none of the notes he or she plays are connected to the pulsating line underneath. It really is remarkable how this conveys the feeling of somebody who is lost, who is "*beklemmt*" [Ed: Beethoven's character designation for this passage, which means pinched, straitened, or even anguished], and it's also remarkable that, having seen this vision of Hell, there would be such a rage that takes place afterward. I always thought of the *Grosse Fuge*, the Great Fugue, as a violent act of nature—not so much in musical terms but as an emotional outbreak.

In his late quartets, Beethoven uses all the traditional forms, such as sonata form, fugue, and ABA song form. But he was also like a scientist or an explorer with his forms. The first movement begins with something that feels like an introduction, but winds up not being an introduction. It winds up being a piece of the puzzle, and what he's done is that he has cut up these different parts of it and keeps on returning to it, and when I thought about it much, much later in my life, it felt like cubist painting in the way it was cut up, and I thought, "how original."

What's going to happen next? Well, the second movement finishes almost before it begins, you know. It's so short, and it's kind of a goofy movement because in the middle there is this clown performing pratfalls, the weirdest sort of joke [bars 50–63]. And then you have this charming and beautiful third movement, with a sort of clippety-cloppety feeling at the beginning. It's almost like a horse ride through the woods. At this point you would think, okay, there are three movements, so there's going to be a last movement to finish this thing off, a brilliant and dazzling fourth movement. But Beethoven was experimenting in all kinds of different ways. So he suddenly turns to this German dance, which is sweetly simple. Not inconsequential, but charming, you know, modest in its goals. *And then!* I wonder whether he planned what happens next or whether he was going on intuition and just thought, "I'll see where this takes me." Because he was quoted as saying that not only in writing the next movement, the Cavatina, but even in thinking about it, he was brought to tears. This is a movement that meant an extraordinary amount to him, but how did he get to that from the first four movements? It's a puzzle, and for me as an eighteen- or nineteen-year-old, it was perplexing to come across this journey he was taking and the journey that as a performer I was taking along with him, but it was also incredibly exciting and moving. And if you think of the Cavatina as a door that opens into another world when it finishes, to me what happens then is a trap door. You're just dropped into this chaos. It's such a shock.

At that time he was homing in on fugues in a most adventurous and fantastic way, having written fugues and double fugues already in the Ninth Symphony, in Op. 110, and in the *Missa Solemnis*. I guess I imagine that he started the *Grosse Fuge* not knowing exactly what was going to happen. First of all, you have this long note. And then he has little bits and pieces of what's to come. He labels the first page as an "overtura," an overture, and it's a bit like a table of contents in a book; as though he is saying that the first chapter is going to be this, the second chapter that, and there's going to be a third and fourth and fifth and sixth chapter. It's almost comical.

SB: You're right. It's so fragmented. First of all, you come out of the ending of the Cavatina, where the first violin descends from E-flat and really tucks in the pitch G [as the third of E-flat]. And then the next thing you know that same G has a thousand volts of electricity surging through it in the very opening of the *Grosse Fuge*. Then there's that crazy angular line, with the trill at the end. And then you get something that sounds like a mechanical "fast forward" operation, played twice (bars 11–16), followed by a very human-sounding thing (bars 17–25).

AS: Yes, as a listener or as a player you're kind of jerked around. After that, you have this wild chaotic thing for several minutes, and then it's as if it runs into a wall and stops, and you have what's a little bit like the eye of the storm (bars 159–233). And then there's another remarkable place where the action stops, and there is a space, and the action tries to move forward again. Then there's another space. It's a little bit like a choo-choo train going along that begins to come back. In a way it's funny, and in another way it's just remarkably odd. Finally it gets back to the fugue subject as a dance, but it doesn't stay a dance for very long. After all this, there are more stops and starts toward the end, where he was saying, "Was I right in this table of contents, in this listing of chapters? Did I get it right?" And then finally, "I think I did." What's wonderful is that the *Grosse Fuge* ends in optimism, in the triumph of a person over this lost soul that he was in the movement before.

SB: Speaking of the last page of the *Grosse Fuge*: how do you land that thing? Because it reminds me of a big jet coming in for a landing. You get the angular theme, but Beethoven normalizes it by bringing it into a more usual, cadential kind of progression.

AS: Yes, it becomes a kind of typical coda at the end.

SB: That last page always sounds extraordinary to me. Perhaps, thinking of your space travel metaphor, this is where we reenter the earth's atmosphere.

AS: Yes, it was space travel, but on the other hand it was also this internal travel that went into areas where some of us are afraid to go. In a way, it's like therapy, you know, when the psychiatrist says, "Don't be afraid. I'm going to lead you into your innermost fears." Beethoven has done that, but I also think that the last movement is something that could be featured on The Weather Channel.

SB: What on earth do you mean?

AS: Because on that channel they're following storms all the time, remarkable acts of nature: tornadoes and things like that. If I had to pick a piece for The Weather Channel it would be the *Grosse Fuge*.

SB: I wanted to pick up on your sense of the rage in the *Grosse Fuge*, because it seems like a plausible reading of the emotional temperature of the thing. What does that feel like when you are playing it, especially that unrelieved stretch of crazy dissonance for however many minutes before, as you say, it hits the wall and then drops into G-flat major, into that more floating section? The sheer dissonance of that first section! No wonder people thought he was crazy.

AS: Do you remember a fad called the primal scream? You were put in a room and you were allowed to scream your head off and get all of the poisons out. Well, this is a little bit like that. I think the best performances of this are when you don't care too much about your sound, you don't care too much about anything except just exploding. It's trying just to let the music explode off the page. And you know, music is often beautiful and civilized, and this is not beautiful, and it's not civilized. It's a shock of reality of another kind. It's real. There's beauty in the world, but there's also torment and strife, and this is it.

It's also interesting to add the unusual thing that happened to this remarkable last movement. There were countless objections to it because it was incomprehensible and outrageous and radical. Beethoven's publisher said, "You can't do this to us. This is impossible."

So he thought about it I think for one day and said, "Okay, I'll write you another piece," and what he wrote was so diametrically opposite. It became the bookend to a sweet piece of music with one remarkable slow movement in it.

SB: In other words, when you replace the *Grosse Fuge* with a more conventional finale, the Cavatina becomes the heart of the matter.

AS: Right.

SB: So why do you think he was willing to let go of the *Grosse Fuge* as the finale? I mean, there's a cynical reason that you hear sometimes, namely that the publisher guaranteed him they would publish a four-hand version of it, so he would still make some money off of it. But I sometimes wonder—do you think he got a sense that the *Grosse Fuge* was indeed overpowering the rest of the quartet? Because he's the guy who, if you told him "Hey, compose that differently," was likely to come back with "How dare you tell me what to do."

AS: That's what I would have expected him to say. "This is my art. How dare you!" The *Grosse Fuge* is almost as long as the four movements that immediately precede it. In this respect, it reminds me of Bach's D Minor Partita for solo violin, because the Chaconne that ends it is unlike anything else he wrote for the violin and is longer than all the four preceding movements put together. There's a theory that Bach wrote the Chaconne because his first wife had died. He came home from a trip to discover that his wife was already dead and buried, and the Chaconne is an expression of his grief. Who knows what was going on in Beethoven's life personally when he composed the *Grosse Fuge*. For one thing, he was not above writing pieces for money. He wrote arrangements of Scottish songs, which are modest, to be kind, but he made a few bucks doing it. And for another thing, he would compose something serious and then turn to something completely different in spirit. I can almost hear him saying, "Enough of that. Let's have some fun."

SB: Yes, he had a remarkable gift for being able to do exactly that. Some people call it romantic irony when artists seem to subvert their own agenda. As when you're in the finale of the Ninth Symphony standing before the radiant throne of God and then the next thing you hear are the bassoons going "blat, blat" on their lowest note. From the sublime to the ridiculous.

AS: In all the times that I played the alternate last movement, I never noticed something that I read about not long ago: that it's possible that a series of notes could be playing games with the notes of the Great Fugue. It's almost the same thing subverted a little bit, as if Beethoven said, "All right, I'm going to write you a sweet piece that has nothing to do with the Great Fugue, but I'm going to play a little game and stick a little something in it that's almost like the fugue theme."

SB: That's fascinating.

AS: Yes, there's a lyrical group of notes that goes around the quartet, and I read somewhere that you could make the case that he was poking fun at all the naysayers to the Great Fugue.

SB: You've said a lot here. When you were describing the *beklemmt* section of the Cavatina, you were giving me goosebumps. Preparing for this interview, I listened to your recordings, and that tone you get in the recording from the '80s during that section is like nothing I've ever heard. It's almost unearthly. It really snaps into focus when you're talking about someone who has lost their way. . . . As you said, the music starts pulsing, and the bass goes down to an unexpected key. You made the astute point that the first violin is not going with the pulse. It's just kind of out there. And that tone that you get—it too is out there, somewhere between reality and imagination.

AS: Well, that was what I was hoping for, trying for. It's interesting: when I coach this piece, and the first violinist comes to that middle section of the cavatina, he or she will often try not to be off with the triplets but to match them, because you're supposed to play together almost always in chamber music, and this is the odd exception. "You want me not to be with everybody else? Are you sure that's what Beethoven wanted?" So they're uncomfortable doing that.

SB: Yes, it goes against the grain. So when you are going to perform the *Grosse Fuge*, what is the locker room chatter about? Is it "Oh God, we've got to get through this thing somehow," or is it like you're going to church, or what? How do you process the *Grosse Fuge* when you actually have to perform it?

AS: Well, you stop being emotional and you start being clinical. We performers often have the sense of turning ourselves into two people: one who has to get it out there to the audience, but then another one who is cold stone sober and says "This has to be louder, this has to be softer," "I did it this way, which means it has to be that way, and the next movement has to stand in comparison," and just planning it out coolly in this manner. Certainly, in rehearsal there is a lot of this kind of planning that has to happen, because if you just let all the voices scream, it's total chaos. What has to happen is that there are primary and secondary voices, which have to be sorted out in a very unemotional way. I remember when our quartet had its fortieth anniversary. Our manager tried to make a little bit of publicity about it and so there was an open rehearsal that was attended by a journalist from Chamber Music America. He called me afterward and said, "I can't write anything about what the rehearsal was like because all you said were things like "two bars after letter B, the viola is not loud enough, and it's a little bit out of tune in the third bar, and then let's make a little bit more of the crescendo." He said, "I need some purple passages from you." But there was nothing, there was absolutely nothing. It was all just "do this here" and "don't do that there." Technical things.

But then there's the magic. As a teacher, I feel that I can't teach the magic. That's innate. Some people have it in one way or another, and other people don't. You could say, "Play this note higher and that one lower" and get an approximation of what might have become magic, but it's not magic.

People often ask me, "Do you miss playing in the Guarneri Quartet and playing string quartets?" I don't. Forty-five years was fantastic, and I'm blessed to have done it. But when I hear young quartets who already play kind of perfectly but don't have that magic, then I think that every single one of my colleagues had that magic.

You know, Michael Tree: nobody sounded like him. John Dalley:

the wonderful detail and imagination that he had, even though it was very subtle. And then David Soyer, who was a swashbuckler, the way he played. He had this devilish way. "I don't care what you think, this is what I think, and I'm going to do it." No sense of caution in his playing. And then Peter Wiley, who succeeded him in the quartet, is this gorgeously artistic player. All these people in our quartet had magic in their playing.

SB: You're lucky.

AS: It's not that I miss it, but I'm certainly grateful to have had the opportunity to hang out with these musicians.

SB: And they with you.

AS: I hope so.

22 Adagio

ROBERT PINSKY

More than midway along, the feeling changes.
The adagio traffic plunges, or else it rises,

From dolent meditation to vibrato chanting.
Want-want, and again, a punctuated longing.

After the stroke, his loss or deafness, or after
The bad election, the movement's harsher or sweeter.

Or one day vowels come out a little distorted
From the thwarted mouth. *Un poco deformato*,

"And yet if it doesn't seem a moment's thwart
Our *pizzicato* stitching and stitching fall short."

Ah *Ma non troppo*: in time the lines returned
For a reprieve, a refrain, the traffic sustained

On the right road, *molto espressivo* redeemed
Between the organ of expression and the mind.

But not so fast—*espressivo* of loss or redemption?
Punishment or joy? Or degrees of each, or neither?

Want-want the cello hums and the waters rise
And fall on the stars and break in years and days.

23 A Long Song Log: Ten Entries on Seriality, to the Accompaniment of Charles Mingus's *Black Saint* (20.i.19–24.i.19)

NATHANIEL MACKEY

"From now on everything I do is gonna be serial," I said at some point, albeit point, pointillism, had gone out into areal disarray the moment I said it. Was it when Dannie Richmond's bass-drum-to-snare-drum-to-sock-cymbal figure, suggestive of two tempos other than its own, gathered and began again for the millionth time as I put Mingus's *The Black Saint and the Sinner Lady* on the box yet again right here on this campus fifty years ago? Point, pointillism, punctuation, wanted to go out, go on. Seriality, it said, allows you to begin again, not to begin only once. It allows you also to begin only once, it said, not to begin again but to resume, to continue. Seriality allows you not to stop. It was beginning to be about time, *Black Saint* said, and beginning was to be about time.

//

"From now on," I said at some point, "everything I do is gonna be serial." Was it when the low brass dredged up graveyard dirt, when bones lined out a sense or a sound of heave or of haul, what Baraka heard in Shepp's horn, "the weight of blackness"? Point asked me if weight was the recursive loop some had been calling history, weight boomeranging yet again as it now boomerangs yet again, our world-historical hurt. If so, it said, seriality is a progressive non-progressive mnemonic we resort to to remind ourselves, inure and inoculate ourselves, a homeopathic vamp-till-ready, a sigh, a pneumatic not-yet.

//

"From now on everything I do is gonna be serial," I said at some point. Point, bleeding outward, elsewhere, whispered (from afar but, even so, audibly), "Seriality is futurity's ghost come back to haunt." Point plotted with curvature to give time a there-before-it-got-there aspect, a not-all-there-but-never-not-there aspect, a sense of untimely expense—hesitation, anticipation—which is nothing if not what seriality is. Seriality is having something, somewhere, to come back to, a kind of home, a close thing to it. Point said we were creatures of time but could we grab hold of it, wield it, swing it. It was something futurity's ghost had said.

//

"From now on everything I do," I said at some point, "is gonna be serial," implicitly aligning "serial" with "funky," *Black Saint*'s recourse to work-song form and sonority saying something about bodily expenditure's waft, honky-tonk hermeneutics getting at something about garter-belt musk, something about the ongoingness of work and desire. Lee Dorsey, I assumed, would approve. Was it Quentin Jackson's trombone claps atop Dannie Richmond's bass-drum-to-snare-drum-to-sock-cymbal figure that effected this alignment or equation at the album's outset? Was it when gray was the color of her dress, then white cotton, in Class of 1938 Hall, that a taste for thirst itself set in, seriality's disavowal of quench or its adherence to an iterative quench? Was it when I knew and was this when I knew I was hearing seriality say it would go my bond? Was it then that a vow "not to anesthetize / desire" took root?

//

At some point I said, "From now on everything I do is gonna be serial." Seriality said, "Abide with me." Seriality took me aside, calling Mingus an avatar of underness and of what would repeatedly be "brought up." I caught point wondering did it all have to do with it, was it all of it, did anything, if it was true form was never more than an extension of content, extend content more than serial form. Point as well wondered, asking out loud, what needed extending more than the lyric, the beleaguered lyric. Call it the long song, the extended lyric, *Black Saint* said, the extended, extenuated lyric. Say-it-again said say it again.

//

"From now on everything I do is gonna be serial," I said at some point. Point said I was like a ghost, latter-day futurity's ghost, haunting the past in "'mu' eighty-second part"—

They were Mrs. Vex and Mr.
Fret but on the box "Me
and Mrs. Jones." 1972 it
might've been... *The*
Black
Saint and the Sinner Lady
followed, "Solo Dancer."
Time leaned in, no matter
when
it might've been. 1963
it might've been... Swank
refrain said to've been
about sex, bodily blare,
lyricless though it was
none-
theless... Nonsonance the
name it got, otherwise wordless, band say nothing
or
it all amount to nothing,
punctual only punctual,
noth-
ing add up

—the all-but-point of origin or the point of all-but-origin *Black Saint* was. Mingus himself had warned: "you don't play the beat where it is.

You draw a picture away from the beat . . . [you] tease the mind by not telling . . . exactly what everyone knows—where one, two, three, and four are." "Away from" founded no polis we knew, the opposition of church to state Mingus's nerve church, nerve-churchicality chanting history down.

//

"From now on everything I do is gonna be serial," I said at some point. Was it when Mingus took a station break during his liner notes? "At this moment I'd like to pause for station identification. Station SOUL and LOVE. Charles Mariano lead alto and alto solos. Jerome Richardson lead baritone, flute, soprano, and baritone solos coming to you through some of these same above stated frequencies plus moral support to yours truly." Was it knowing not everyone wanted to know what love was, what soul was, that did it? We would forever be identifying our station as the dial drifted and we played beset by static. Seriality, point put in, is an advance of parts leaning on one another, mutually supporting, wanting to say what would not be known otherwise, otherwise not be known, an interplay of parts. Was it that, taken with Mingus's lush, night-on-the-town romanticism, his erotic-elegiac romanticism, a knowing romantic toss and return, one knew one would never be done being put thru love's paces, by which time one seemed, even to oneself, to be point personified. Point said I was a phased, epiepiphanous ghost visiting the future in " 'mu' two hundred thirtieth part": "Her black saint I'd be, the two of / us / abed in black sheets, black satin, satanic accents / never not near." Seriality, *Black Saint* said, is the interrogated lyric striking back, a suspect bittersweetness taking its time. Say-it-again said it again.

//

"From now on," I said at some point, "everything I do is gonna be serial." Point preceded but found support in C. S. Giscombe's *Giscome Road*, whose "long song" is "a bridge of horns," "a commotion w/ out words / about the contempt for arrival / all about the taste for arrival," a mixed-emotional road song, a ridden song, a song of transit. The long song pursues but only ostensibly pursues arrival, eschewing arrival, a dissident song disavowing arrival, as if, black, to say, sizing up the New World, "Look at where arrival got us." Even Columbus, in Kamau Brathwaite's extended, extenuated lyric, his long song *The Arrivants*, is given pause:

> Columbus from his after-
> deck saw bearded fig trees, yellow pouis
> blazed like pollen and thin
>
> waterfalls suspended in the green
> as his eyes climbed towards the highest ridges
> where our farms were hidden.
>
> Now he was sure
> he heard soft voices mocking in the leaves.
> What did this journey mean, this
>
> new world mean: dis-
> covery? Or a return to terrors
> he had sailed from, known before?

The long song is seriality's far side, seriality's dream of wholeness deferred, the blutopic interanimation of wonder and rue that Giscombe says "edges in & in it I'd shout":

> The long song's nameless though and invisible this or this loomed among the trees as it repeated: it crawled & rued its day & crawled & came repeatedly to its own lips rueing its day:
>
> the return to the sites was not sweet,
> back out was not familiar-sounding the second time through or the third,
> the return was aloof itself

Point felt itself apart from itself. It recognized a holding of arrival's repeat at arm's length, a being off to the side. Point preceded Giscombe but followed Mingus when Robert Kelly said fashion teaches brevity but brevity, he was sorry to say, is a lie, "I must be longer with this music"—another way of saying, as I had at some point, "From now on everything I do is gonna be serial." Still, point wanted to know why "w/ out words," why "nameless." There's a music, I answered, a long song, an extended, extenuated lyric that's beyond rendering, rending, rendition. Seriality chases it.

//

"From now on everything I do is gonna be serial," I said at some point. Was it during the 11:30–11:59 stretch on side two of *Black Saint*, when one realized the earlier 06:31–07:00 stretch had been an adumbration, an anticipatory, cut-short taste of what was to come, the full extension to be heard beginning at 11:30 hinted at but interrupted, held back? One heard that one had heard a hesitant tack having to do with having to wait, with asking "How long?" perhaps, a lush, rhapsodic windup whose delivery had been deferred, a tack betokening the tease it might all, after all, be. At 11:59 that delivery began to unfold, where rhapsody was an etymologically understood stitching alongside everything else it was (night-on-the-town romanticism, erotic-elegiac romanticism, bright lights, low city, low but lit city, etc.). Was it during the five-and-a-half-minute bacchanal starting at 11:59, the all-out, sixty-minute-man locomotion that takes the piece out, with its return to Dannie Richmond's bass-drum-to-snare-drum-to-sock-cymbal figure and the tuba's low croak, a rhapsodic hectoring, and to the piece's opening theme at the end? That the end is a beginning, the beginning an end, was it one was to take it, point wanted to know, that there's a certain circularity to seriality's deferred wholeness? Again calling me latter-day futurity's ghost, point said I myself had said or implied as much in "'mu' one hundred thirty-second part"—

A certain someone's deep audition, whose name
he resorted to. Dark light, dark box of light.
Light nowhere to be found. A baby dead in the
back-
seat of a car, airstrikes on Gaza, the world on
the TV screen... What world romance would

remake were it able, whatsee's knife in the
eye. The world romance would remake were they
ro-
mantic, not that they were that anymore... Love
had a way of moving on they'd heard and were
learning, home had a way of leaving too. Home,
they
now saw, was a certain hesitation, again as in the
begin-
ning but beginning, gap the world gathered
in

—a ghost scavenging old and new ground. Point, swayed by Jay Berliner's flamenco guitar's repeated entrances, broke loose and foraged, rummaging the world. Writing, H.D. said, wants to go on. Seriality wants to even more.

//

"From now on," I said at some point, "everything I do is gonna be serial." An after-the-fact pre-post-expectancy. A low-lit, slow-drag ebullience. Disconsolate creatures of time but could we swing it. There had to've been a point, an exact when. Could happening upon, by way of Robert Creeley, Parmenides's relativization of point, his near dismissal of point, *Black Saint* made me wonder, have been that when, that point? "It is all one to me where I begin," I had read and now heard echoing as I listened to *Black Saint*, "for I shall come back there again." Was that when? And as our latter-day Mingus, Henry Threadgill, asked a while back: When was that?

24 Ghazal for the End of Time

JANE HIRSHFIELD

(*after Messiaen*)

Break anything—a window, a pie crust, a glacier—it will break open.
A voice cannot speak, cannot sing, without lips, teeth, *lamina propria*
coming open.

Some breakage can barely be named, hardly be spoken.
Rains stopped, roof said. Fires, forests, cities, cellars peeled open.

Tears stopped, eyes said. An unhearable music fell instead from them.
A clarinet stripped of its breathing, the cello abandoned.

The violin grieving, a hand too long empty held open.
The imperial piano, its 89th, 90th, 91st strings unsummoned, unwoken.

Watching, listening, was like that: the low, wordless humming of being
unwoven.
Fish vanished. Bees vanished. Bats whitened. Arctic ice opened.

Hands wanted more time, hands thought we had time. Spending time's
rivers,
its meadows, its mountains, its instruments tuning their silence, its
deep mantle broken.

Earth stumbled within and outside us.
Orca, thistle, kestrel withheld their instruction.

Rock said, Burning Ones, pry your own blindness open.
Death said, Now I too am orphan.

25 Spaces for Music

FRANK GEHRY

Interviewed by Mark Swed

Los Angeles–based music critic Mark Swed has interviewed the renowned architect Frank Gehry on many occasions. For this particular interview, they spoke together on April 25, 2018, for more than an hour at the Gehry Studios in Los Angeles. What follows is an edited transcript of their discussion, which began with Gehry describing the role of music in his childhood and early adulthood. His mother had studied violin and took him to many concerts throughout his youth; his sister played the harp and married composer Morton Subotnick; and he cultivated music with friends both in high school and later at USC. Throughout his early career as an architect, he met with a number of prominent musicians, including Pinchas Zukerman, Zubin Mehta, and Pierre Boulez. The conversation then turned to Gehry's concert halls and the special relationship of his architecture to performers and audiences.

It may be helpful to clarify some of the references that occur in the interview: the Dorothy Chandler Pavilion is the former home of the LA Philharmonic; Ernest Fleischmann is the former executive director of the LA Philharmonic and Esa-Pekka Salonen the former music director; the orchestra pit designed for Disney Hall had not been realized when Peter Sellars's production of *Don Giovanni*, with sets by Gehry, was performed there; MTT is Michael Tilson Thomas—he and Gehry collaborated in the design of the New World Center in Miami; Daniel is Daniel Barenboim, the pianist and conductor who commissioned the Boulez Saal; Frank Gehry was born Frank Owen Goldberg; and the tower Gehry did in New York is known as New York by Gehry.

MS: How did the presence of music and musicians in your personal life lead to the vision you had about the way you could create spaces that would change how music is perceived, both the music itself but also the social condition around it? Walt Disney Concert Hall in particular, but every one of your halls has produced that kind of transformative experience.

FG: It's about people. Architecture is a stage set, as Shakespeare called it, but it's not thought of that way enough. I had so many bad experiences giving lectures in universities and places where the halls were just not friendly. You got up and you didn't feel the audience. I'm sure you've experienced that. But it doesn't have to be that way. It's easy to fix. You just have to think about the idea of making a connection between audience and performer. When we were doing Disney, I didn't know our acoustician, Yasuhisa Toyota, well in the first round. He was much younger and cautious about testing his own relationship to the architecture. He knew there was an acoustic relationship, but he didn't know how to talk about it. As we got to know each other and talked about the relationship of people and acoustics, I finally got him to admit there was a component, which he called psychoacoustics, that had to be addressed. At the time of Disney Hall, he acknowledged that it's about thirty-five percent of the game. Now I think he's up to fifty percent. We've really talked through this stuff, the nitty-gritty of it, and I don't think he has had that from other architects who are not as involved with music as I am.

MS: And what is that nitty-gritty? Is it the idea that the environment of a concert hall profoundly influences the way you hear something?

FG: Right, the physical space is going to affect your experience, and it could make it unpleasant. There's a new hall that I just went to. When you close your eyes, the sound is great. But when you open your eyes, it's precarious. I've seen that a lot, and it doesn't take much to really think that through. Yasu and I really have a good relationship and a good way to talk about it now.

MS: *How* do you talk about it? It's just as important for the performers as for the audience, right? Toyota has told me that a concrete wall, for example, might have the same reflective properties as hard wood, but it doesn't look like it does. So performers tend to play in such a way as to compensate for that difference by, say, the strings adding more vibrato to warm up the sound. These things can affect everybody.

FG: You have to create a collaborative relationship with the orchestra and an environment that deals with their issues. A lot of stuff goes on under the covers with the orchestra. In designing Disney, I watched the stagehands setting up for a concert in the Dorothy Chandler Pavilion many times. I watched what they did and talked to the players about it. I talked to Ernest Fleischmann about it. It became obvious that certain members of the orchestra didn't like to sit next to other certain members. They weren't compatible socially. That's just the way people are. They would get stagehands to move their seat three inches this way or that so that they weren't in the face of a guy who was known to have eaten garlic before he got on stage.

MS: Did you also deal with musical issues for the orchestra stage setup?

FG: I asked Ernest whether we could go somewhere and set up the orchestra the way then music director Esa-Pekka Salonen thinks he'd like it. So Ernest got Royce Hall for a day. We set it up, and Salonen moved the seats around. Over a four- or five-hour span, he got things going the way he wanted and said, "That's it." So we measured it and built new risers in the Chandler, which got a rave review from a critic who hated Ernest and the orchestra. He reluctantly said, "What happened?" It looked better, too. It was orderly. Eventually, we had to make some adjustments because it was letter-perfect to what we wanted, but it needed some humanity. We had some human issues that had to be dealt with. So we moved things around a little bit, I'd say like ten percent, and the orchestra got used to it. That's what became the exact model for the risers in Disney Hall.

MS: Do you always start from the human and the musical side like that when you're thinking about building for music?

FG: I'm no music scholar, so I have to take my direction or feelings from hanging around and listening to musicians. I listen to Peter

Sellars talking about [Wagner's] *Tristan*. I listen to Esa-Pekka talking to Peter Sellars. I listen to members of the orchestra. I listen in rehearsals whenever I can. You get a lot of information from that. Disney Hall has an orchestra pit built into the design that would serve very well for opera and other stuff Peter Sellars has done. If we had the orchestra pit for *Don Giovanni*, it would have been great. The idea of having an orchestra pit in a classical music concert hall should not be thought of as an extra, as it is when they get to budget cutting. We don't need that. But the other thing that we've messed with is the film thing. We messed with that with MTT in Miami. Because it is an institution for teaching, and because MTT is the curious critter he is, we were able to explore things like that.

MS: But what about the inclusion of surfaces for video projections, which you designed into the shape of that hall?

FG: On opening night, they performed Thomas Adès's *Polaris* with added video. The visuals were beautiful, and the music was equally beautiful. But the two had nothing to do with each other, and so finally I just had to close my eyes. That issue is confronting the music world as it builds new concert halls. What do you do about that? You can get a surround visual if you want it, but do you really want it? Then the music has to be written for that.

MS: I would imagine the last thing you want when you're thinking about a concert hall is a place where people close their eyes.

FG: Yes, I would hope that we create some place that enriches the experience.

MS: One thing I find curious is that for all your avant-garde spirit as an artist and all you've accomplished for new music, especially with Disney, the New World Center, and the magical new Pierre Boulez Saal in Berlin, you have also said that your real love is eighteenth-, nineteenth- and early twentieth-century music, not the avant-garde. Is that true?

FG: Not completely. But that's my comfort zone. I don't always get it with new pieces and have to go back and listen again. But even though I'm used to listening to Pierre's music, for instance, it doesn't involve me emotionally like the *Goldberg Variations*, for instance, do. I like it. I like the idea of it. I like the structure of it. But I wouldn't cry in such a piece. It has a different feeling.

MS: You yourself have commissioned new work, particularly from Salonen, who you had hoped would write a piece for Bilbao when it was built, but he never got around to it. Now you're part of a group commissioning an opera from him.

FG: I simply like being around musicians. I like going to concerts. When it comes to the pieces I like, I love Chopin's piano music a lot. I love Mahler's First Symphony, which Salonen conducted recently. There are a lot of works I can get excited about. But I'd say piano is number one on the hit parade. I really get off on listening to it. I love András Schiff when he comes.

MS: Is it the performer who draws you in? Who else besides Schiff?

FG: I'm trying to rearrange my life so I can be in LA when Mitsuko Uchida plays. I couldn't be in Berlin for her. I wanted so much to hear her play in the Boulez Saal. She's on my telephone ring tone. It's Beethoven. Once it rang when I was in Berlin with Daniel. It rang, and he recognized it. He said, "Frank, I should be on your ringer." When Pierre conducted Ravel, I would go crazy.

MS: Different as these performers are, they all share a commitment to great clarity and structure. The architecture of the piece is the key component. Do you think that has something to do with it?

FG: I don't know. I like that there's a pattern.

MS: Do you think about music in architectural terms? Do you think about the structure?

FG: I used to. When we were in school, I used to have Bach on all of the time, because with Bach you can feel the structure. You could derive Mies van der Rohe right from it.

MS: So when you have called the *Goldberg Variations* your favorite piece, that isn't just a joke on your name? It's really because the piece is of incredible structural interest to you?

FG: It does mean a lot to me other than for the funny reason. I'm even on the Glenn Gould Foundation. I love listening to Gould's early recording of the *Goldberg Variations* and then his late recording. It's beautiful, the difference. And, of course, then you hear all the different people who play it.

MS: Now that you have been working long enough to have had an early, middle, and late career yourself, do you view your work like that as well? Just as with Gould's early and late *Goldbergs*, there's a much greater expansiveness and warmth to your later buildings than when you were an edgy young radical.

FG: Maybe it has something to do with that. I never thought of that. It makes some sense. I think when you start out, the good thing is that you're alone. If you're doing it right, you're the only expert. What anybody else says doesn't mean anything. That's just an opinion. I've lived by that. I got a lot of shit from people when I started, mostly architects, who later became friends. We all have. You get jealous when someone gets ahead of you on something. There's a lot of something to prove. You push things, and there is just a little bit more anger in the game. There was something about the detailing I did that drove people crazy.

MS: That detailing has always been a key element in what you do. And it's a key element in music. Do you see a connection?

FG: You get all this variety from [just a few notes], and it's the same in architecture. We're using wood and metal and plaster and some other stuff. The variety is in what you do with it. The tower I did in New York is next to the Woolworth Building and near the Brooklyn Bridge; you can see them together. So I carefully designed the building with the scale of the elements that were similar to the scale of the architecture of that period. The Woolworth Building has a terra cotta solid piece on the outside that goes down and the windows between, and I scaled the metal that I was using to that dimension. The Woolworth Building has a stair step. You go up a certain height, and you step back. I did the same. I used that language. If you look at the picture of that, you feel the relationship of that ensemble. And that's what I am trying to do in Toronto with the skyscraper I'm designing. Those buildings I did fit with the historicist buildings. I mean, they're not historicist, but they have the body language. In composing the image, I have those pieces, and I can put them together, so it's like the notes in music.

MS: Is this then a visual worldview of composition that has an analogue in music?

FG: I can't read music, but I look at the score and I can see that Pierre's score is different from Chopin's score. You can feel the drift. You can feel that there's something going on, and I suspect if I spent the time looking at it, I'd pick up a structure or cadence in it without knowing what it meant.

MS: How much, if any, does your personal friendship with musicians influence the way you think about structure?

FG: What's useful to me is when I think about the differences between Gustavo Dudamel and Esa-Pekka. I was trained for eighteen years by Esa-Pekka. Then Gustavo comes in with his Tchaikovsky, and I couldn't stand it. I thought, "Oh God, this is going to be terrible for me." But my wife is Latin. I understand the Latin tempo and feeling. So there are these differences. I am recognizing differences. I always need it to be a personal relationship.

MS: Was it also something personal that drew you to Gagaku, the ancient Japanese court music? It seems a strange love of yours.

FG: When I was a student, the teaching of architecture in LA was very Asia-centric. All the professors at USC had been to Japan in the war, and they talked about the architecture they had seen all the time. Japan was a big deal, and some of my early works look very Japanese. Even stuff I still do has a feeling of wood and Asia. So it was important for me to study the literature, the art. I really got into the woodcuts and Hiroshige and the Edo period screens. Greg Walsh and I actually curated a Japanese art show way back. And since I was into all of it culturally, I wanted to focus musically, too. My sister was at UCLA playing the harp in the UCLA Orchestra, and Doreen told me the ethnomusicology department had a Gagaku orchestra I should listen to.

MS: You wound up joining the orchestra.

FG: I got a frame with a frying pan and two mallets and would go "clink clink." And they sent a guy from Japan to teach me how to breathe, and I found out there was a dance that went with it, but only saw pictures of the dance. Years later, I went to Japan and actually saw it. Have you ever seen it? It's quiet and I *loved* it. It was so architectural and it was so accessible to me.

MS: So actually your only real music training was Gagaku.

FG: Well, no, there's a secret one I'll tell you about, but let's finish Gagaku.

MS: Okay.

FG: I loved it and spent a lot of time with it, and then, I don't know, I got busy with architecture and it all disappeared until Disney was built. I was with Yasu Toyota at a dinner that the Japanese consul gave in LA for us. After a lot of sake, the Japanese consul said, "Mr. Gehry, we love your work. What can we do for you?" I didn't understand when he said, "What can we do for you." I had had enough sake. I said, "Yeah, I'll tell you what you can do for me." I said, "Could you bring a Gagaku orchestra?" I knew they never traveled anywhere; I was just drunk and pushing it. We left and then months later he called and said, "I've arranged it." Only about 900 people showed up for the concert, but [the orchestra and dancers] made Disney Hall look like a Japanese temple. As soon as you put them in, boom.

MS: What about your musical secret?

FG: My secret music career started in Timmins, Ontario, when I was eight years old. We had a cousin who was the radio announcer at the Timmins radio station. My mother wanted me to do something musical. My parents didn't have any money, but through one of my father's businesses, they found a guy who taught Hawaiian guitar. So I went to lessons. They bought me a Hawaiian guitar, one of those metal things, with picks and stuff. I learned to play "Aloha," and my cousin with the radio station got me on the air playing "Aloha." That's my musical career.

MS: Are there any other ways in which music has had an effect on your work?

FG: I drop everything to go to concerts.

26 Going Spatial

LAURIE ANDERSON
AND EDGAR CHOUEIRI

I

Bach's Mass in B Minor, Schütz's Passion motets, Lou Reed's "Pale Blue Eyes," Umm Kulthum's chanting of the surah of Abraham, every Georges Brassens song, Led Zeppelin's first two notes on their first album: Our favorite musical bits are erasure-proof memories, pleasurable recollections we can conjure up with a mere tap on an audio player. We like to talk about them, see something of ourselves in them, and share them with kindred spirits. We do so with the subliminal hope of reaffirming, or furthering, a connection, like a light kiss on a willing cheek. We think of this book as a string of such kisses.

But in every composer and technologist hides a futurist, and the futurist in the two of us is more anxious to anticipate than to contemplate. So instead of talking about the music we love, we set out to imagine a music yet to be made.

With one hundred and thirty million tracks in the Gracebook database, a melophobic mathematician steeped in the theory of permutations might provocatively ask: What music remains to be made? We like to retort that music, far from stalling in flight, may be just about to make a big leap into a new space, or more specifically, a leap *into* space—3D space that is. Music is going spatial.

Spatial music is music in which the spatial aspect of sound—the perceived location, extent, and movements of sound sources in surrounding space—is more or less equal in stature to the traditional aspects, or elements, of music—pitch, timbre, texture, volume/dynamics, attack/duration/decay, melody, rhythm, and form. We shall call this traditional aspect of music *canonical* and contrast it with the *spatial*.

Our daily experience of sound outside of music is rich in the spatial aspect and poor in the canonical. We constantly hear sounds localized or moving in 3D space but most sounds—the engine rattle of a passing bus, the rustle of tree leaves in the park, even a melodic birdsong—heard one day are not easily hummable in the shower the next. In most music the opposite has been true: We hum and remember the melodies and we sway to the rhythms, but we have grown to accept that the spatial location and extent of musical sounds and their movement in space are, at most, secondary to the canonical elements. We are thus as oblivious to the music that is constantly unfolding in natural space as we have been unfazed by the lack of spatial sound in music.

The spatial "color" has largely been missing from the composer's palette, due, no doubt, solely to technical difficulties—having a violinist float untethered into the sky, a singer whisper in your ear, the crash of cymbals accelerate toward you from all directions. It is as if the color red were always missing from the painter's palette for solely technical reasons (say, nature somehow made it difficult to extract red pigment from the many red things around us), ergo all paintings in our museums have not a hue of red and we have grown accustomed to this incongruence between nature and art.

The incongruence between the abundance of the spatial color in nature and the lack of it in the art of music has unsettled and motivated more than one pioneering composer, from the earliest days of antiphony to the computer age. These experimentalists strived and struggled feverishly. They chopped choirs into pieces and strewed them around the church (Palestrina); immersed bewildered congregations with sound from enthralling rings of singers (Striggio, Tallis); prescribed voices to move along dramatic trajectories on a stage (Monteverdi); sliced the orchestra into layers of spatial polyphony spread over the concert hall (Ives) and even a whole city (Brant); filled large cavernous spaces with synthetized sounds from hundreds of loudspeakers (Varèse); and, bordering on the absurd, even got a string quartet to circle a stadium in four helicopters (Stockhausen)! These attempts and experiments show that the idea of spatial music is not new. They also reflect as much pioneering inventiveness as, perhaps, frustration with the lack of tools that could allow the rendering of the spatial in music as freely and dynamically as its rendering in nature. Had Palestrina the technology and tools to levitate his prepubescent sopranos to flutter like angels high in the church's apse, wouldn't he have done it?

Could it be that such tools are finally here?

Indeed, recently matured audio technologies and techniques with intimidating names such as "wave field synthesis," "higher-order ambisonics," "auralization," and "crosstalk cancellation," fueled by the quest for augmented reality (AR), are just emerging from research laboratories around the world. They are promising to enable music to make its long-heralded spatial leap—to add the missing "red" to the palette of music making.

It is in this context that the two of us set out to celebrate the advent of these tools and imagine a music yet to be made.

We first sat in a beautiful and venerable library and tried to play armchair theorists. We set ourselves the mental exercise of imagining what it takes to create, now that it seems technically feasible, a piece of music in which the canonical is almost completely suppressed in favor of the spatial—music with virtually no melody or rhythm or traditional orchestration, but which works, i.e., gives pleasure, through purely spatial effects. We quickly realized that we badly lacked the vocabulary, the aesthetic framework if you will, to describe the character of such music let alone the ability to prescribe its laws. Formulating laws of composition is the sober work of theorists, and neither of us fancied ourself a real theorist, but honing a new vocabulary is more in the impish realm of songsmiths and playful poets—the stakes may be lower but more is the fun and the worst that could happen is that few would hum our song. So, we opted for the lighter quest and, with unburdened spirit, left the venerable library, crossed the street, and walked into a softly lit restaurant.

II

The restaurant was new in the neighborhood, and it featured an exacting Italian chef intent on crafting new dishes using American ingredients and elements of the cuisine of the Veneto region, from where he hails. Learning that our chef was also on a quest to hone a new vocabulary of sorts, we felt kindred to him and his kitchen, from which flowed a string of sublime dishes that seemed as verses of one poem. Enchanted, exhorted, and with our sense of grandiosity fortified by a heady Corvina wine, we echoed that culinary versification, dish by dish, with one of our own: a list of elements for a tentative aesthetical framework for spatial music! Hours later, by the time the seventh and last dish was brought out, we had minted the last of our list of seven elements. The complete list was: Reverb; Envelopment; Depth & Proximity; Spatial Extent & Resolution; Motion; Spatial Modulation; and Spatial Segregation.

What follows is our attempt to argue that these seven elements, despite their technical-sounding names, can be understood easily and intuitively, and that they can constitute a natural framework to talk about the spatial aspect of music, at least until we stand corrected by a scrupulous scholar or a diligent graduate student.

Each discussion that eventually led us, albeit circuitously, to stumble on, and define, one of these cardinal elements (highlighted in bold letters below) was triggered by something one of us told the other.

HAVE YOU HEARD THE TROY SAVINGS BANK?

Laurie asked this question with so much awe in her voice that one would think she was referring to a new Caruso. But how could one hear a space, let alone a savings bank?

When someone claps once in an enclosed space, a listener in that space first hears the direct sound; then, a few milliseconds later, the sound of the clap having reflected off a nearby surface, arrives again, a bit softer, at the ear of the listener. Other reflections of the clap are in turn reflected again, and again, before reaching the listener's ears. It is those numerous later reflections, which reach the ears almost randomly from all directions and fuse into a sort of pleasant, soft, and quickly decaying din, that we call **reverb**, and that give the space its acoustic identity. The Troy Savings Bank happens to have a beautiful reverb—the most stunning that Laurie, who performed there, had ever heard. But what makes a space's reverb "beautiful" to humans? Reverb, Edgar speculated, gives us the reassuring sense that we are safely cocooned in a protective space, like that of our ancestral caves. With no reverb, which would be the case in open air, we tend to feel exposed. On the other hand, when the later reflections that make up the reverb "tail" of the sound reach the left and right ears at the same time (acousticians, in their particular parlance, call this "reverb with high inter-aural correlation"), which would be the case in, say, a squash court or the symmetric corner of a room, we tend to feel anxious, perhaps a subconscious reminder of a primordial fear, like that of being trapped in a corner of the cave. There seems to be a sweet spot (the holy grail of concert hall acousticians) between no reverb and a highly symmetric one ("highly correlated"), where humans are most seduced by sound. With this much emotional and aesthetic impact, reverb deserves first place in our List of Seven.

THE SINGING TREES OF BASEL

Reverb is often enveloping, "like a diffusing perfume," Laurie (whose late husband once concocted a scent of gasoline and leather) mused. But sound envelopment does not require reverb. One can be as effectively enveloped by *direct* (i.e., non-reverberant) sound. As if to illustrate this part of our dinner conversation, Laurie a few years before conceived and constructed a number of trees for a park in Basel where each tree was filled with many tiny speakers, like leaves, all emitting the same cicada-like chirp. Walking among the trees, the listener is surrounded by sweeping and enveloping patterns of sound. The piece thus eschewed the canonical and relied solely on the spatial for its evocative and meditative power, in particular on a single spatial element: **envelopment**, which takes the runner-up place on our List.

"AND THE LOCUSTS SANG, OFF IN THE DISTANCE"

Nature itself has been staging, in the eastern United States, a long-running series of enveloping cicada-tree-concerts of its own (even longer running than Princeton's 125-year-old concert series!) following a very specific and peculiar schedule: every seventeen years. Every seventeen years, on a spring evening, with uncanny and primeval synchronicity, the aptly named magicicada nymphs emerge from the ground, in millions, climb up trees, molt, and the males among them form choruses that sing a mating song for weeks in an almost deafening unison. Spatial music critics agree that their last performance (in 2004) was lackluster. They barely showed up—harbinger of a brewing lament from a tormented Earth? But Edgar fondly remembers the performance of 1987: "It was impossible to have a conversation under my maple tree." In 1970, they set up a tremendous show in the majestic white ashes that surround Nassau Hall, to inspire Bob Dylan, who came to Princeton to receive an honorary doctorate, to write his *Day of the Locusts* song: "And the locusts sang, off in the distance / Yeah, the locusts sang such a sweet melody." Dylan, the eternal bard, heard the cicadas "off in the distance," chanting high up in the grand domed canopies, and it sounded sweet. But step under a diminutive dogwood on the day of the locusts and the unnerving cicada shrills are more those of a biblical infestation. The difference? **Proximity**. Proximity, our third spatial element, is a powerful emotive tool that can work on its own, as in our day of the locusts example, or as a catalyst when combined with that old canonical element, volume: Proximity + High Volume = Threat; Proximity + Low Volume = Whisper. These two equations do not hold well without proximity, since high volume by itself from a distance is not threatening, nor can low volume by itself from a distance invoke a whisper. Proximity is a corollary of spatial depth, and to be more inclusive we shall call our third element **depth & proximity**.

THE MAN WHO CAPTURED THE SEA

Laurie recalled, "Bob Bielecki came to visit. He set up an unassuming playback array of forty-eight small one-dollar speakers in a line, which he used to play a 48-track recording he did with an equal number of microphones. There was no processing, nothing fancy. The recording was of waves on the seashore." She paused, and whispered, "It was the most amazing representation of space. It did not surround you, but had a mid and a front. It *presented* itself to you." It did not take us too many sips of wine to figure out that Laurie's rapture can be traced to two related fundamental elements: **spatial extent & resolution**. Extent, quite distinct from envelopment, is the perception that the sound occupies a three-dimensional volume like a hologram, unlike the soundstage of regular stereo playback, where the sound is confined to a thin layer of space (a so-called phantom image) between two speakers. Resolution, on the other hand, is the extent to which detail and structure can be discerned within that extent. Bob's feat, despite his rudimentary technique (technically, it is the simplest implementation of a method called "wave field synthesis"), also hints at something fundamental that is contentious enough to be better left as a question: If an array of cheap speakers that obviously lack *tonal* accuracy can capture the realism and *presence* of the sea more than an expensive and tonally accurate system that lacks *spatial* accuracy (say, an audiophile stereo system), doesn't that hint at the superiority of the spatial realm over the canonical one?

"GRANDIOSE ABSURDIST ENTERTAINMENT"

Thus was Stockhausen's *Helicopter String Quartet*, spatial music's most infamous attempt at **motion**, judged by Alex Ross, the *New York Times* music critic, on its premiere in 1995. One suspects that even such daredevils of the canonical realm as Stravinsky and Schoenberg, among others, fearing such brutal critical judgment, shied away from composing for the marching band in favor of perfectly stationary players. But now that new tools allow panning, projecting, and *moving* sounds anywhere in 3D space, motion becomes another hue of that once-elusive "red pigment." A sound accelerating fast along a trajectory in space can leave us as breathless as can an increasing tempo. So, motion is to the spatial what tempo is to the canonical, and much more. While spatial motion, speed, and acceleration can pack as much emotive punch as their canonical counterparts (e.g., *accelerando* and *ritardando*), motion in space can do something tempo simply can't: modulate the very pitch of sound. ("Modulate" is just a fancy word for modify.) The textbook example is the Doppler effect, which makes every passing train's whistle a delightful two-tone *glissando*.

THEY BOUNCED THE MOONLIGHT SONATA OFF THE MOON

The Doppler effect is an example of motion in space modulating (the pitch of) sound, but space *itself* can directly modulate sound—many aspects of musical sound. A flute is an example of space (i.e., the space inside a hollow tube with holes) modulating pitch, and in a very similar way, a living room's space and walls modulate the bass component of sound by setting up a wondrous stationary pattern of sound (called standing waves). Play a pipe organ recording in that room, and when you walk into that standing wave pattern you will hear the bass notes magically disappear or become deafening depending where you walk. **Spatial modulation** is an almost infinite trove of numerous magical effects that go by scientific and poetic names like dispersion, diffraction, refraction, reflection, absorption, resonance, feedback, amplification, and evanescence. Laurie reminisced about experiments with ethereal guitar *feedback* in monumental spaces. Edgar waxed about a sensitive instrument in his rocket lab that, thanks to a serendipitous *resonance*, picked up from forty miles inland the sound of the ocean deep rocking the New Jersey land mass. The concept of spatial modulation of sound is so visceral to nature that the mathematical equation that describes it—the fundamental "wave equation"—is essentially the same one that describes the structure of the atom. Until very recently, the key to that trove of spatial modulations effects was not available, and not a single aspect of this richest of the spatial elements could make it into any of Beethoven's works. As if to redress the wrong and usher the maestro into the spatial realm, the Scottish artist Katie Paterson coded the "Moonlight" Sonata into radio waves, shot them at the Moon, where they *diffracted* around craters, *dispersed* on the surface, then *reflected* back to Earth and were decoded into electrical signals that drove a player piano. Laurie heard it. She described it as "exquisitely fractured."

WHAT IVES WAS UP TO

A proof that theorists are sometimes useful is a classic book with the clinical sounding title *Auditory Scene Analysis* by the Gestalt psychologist Albert Bregman. There we learn about the perceptual phenomenon of **spatial segregation**,[5] through which a listener's ability to unravel the content of complex auditory signals is enhanced when

5 Bregman calls this "spatial masking," but we find this term a bit opaque in the context of spatial music.

the signals are spatially segregated. In its musical analogue, spatial segregation helps us unravel convoluted melodic and rhythmic composition much like adding color to the strands of a complex braid helps us better perceive its structure. Here is a little thought experiment that illustrates spatial segregation in music: Take a Bach three-voice fugue and have it played by three pianists on three separate pianos placed far apart in a large hall, instead of on the single keyboard it was intended for. A listener now has the ability to lock in on one voice and effectively "mute" (or "mask," to use Bregman's term) the other two at will, much as one at a cocktail party can mute everyone but one's object of focus, irrespective of distance. Granted that is not what one ought do to a Bach fugue, but for a complex polyphonic work spatial segregation could act like shining revealing spotlights on an amorphous scene.

A proof that composers don't have to wait for the formalized insight of theorists to make a breakthrough is that Charles Ives, well before Bregman's seminal 1990 book, relied precisely on spatial segregation when he spatially separated subgroups of a symphony orchestra to better reveal his complex polyphony. There is poetic justice in liberating the oppressed: the spatial, once liberated, far from displacing its historical oppressor the canonical, acts with benevolence to enhance it.

And so we added spatial segregation to our little glossary for going spatial.

III

When the Corvina grapes had imparted all their spirit, and the kitchen had gone dark and quiet, we stepped out into the brisk Manhattan night clasping our List of Seven Elements.

Suddenly, we were both struck by the suspicion that someone had somehow beaten us to the List, for, as we reached the avenue, we were immersed in a sort of spatial sonata, with envelopment, depth, proximity, extent, resolution, modulation and motion, even down to the Doppler effect!: A taxi driver, speeding down the avenue in his empty yellow cab, elbow out the window, his taxi light off, anxious to get home, blew by us and, like a trilling nightingale grazing a startled traveler, splashed us with the sounds of his favorite Urdu music.

Acknowledgments

Ways of Hearing was greatly enhanced by the efforts of some very special people. The editors would like to thank Princeton University Concerts both for crucial financial support and for ongoing encouragement. Lisa Tkalych and Henry Valoris provided indispensable organizational assistance in the early stages of this project, and the poetic sensibilities of Dasha Koltunyuk and Tom Uhlein helped us establish the look and feel of the volume. We happily acknowledge the services of copyeditor Jodi Beder and indexer Fred Kameny, and we are also very grateful for the energy and enthusiasm of the editorial and production staff at Princeton University Press, notably including Anne Savarese, Jill Harris, and Jodi Price.

Contributors

LAURIE ANDERSON's boundless creative passions—as visual artist, composer, poet, photographer, filmmaker, electronics whiz, inventor, vocalist, and instrumentalist—make her one of the most compelling artistic forces of our time. An icon of performance art whose prolific work has influenced most corners of contemporary culture, her pioneering spirit has transformed the modern understanding of language and storytelling within the arts.

JAMIE BARTON made her way from a small town in the foothills of the Appalachian Mountains to the stages of the world's most prestigious opera houses. The sensational mezzo-soprano has also extended her voice and charisma to speak up for women, queer people, and other marginalized communities.

DAPHNE A. BROOKS is Professor of African American Studies, Theater Studies, and American Studies at Yale University—and a rock music critic on the side. Her work, rooted in the transformative power of the arts, examines popular music culture through the lens of race, gender, sexuality, and performance.

EDGAR CHOUEIRI is a professor of applied physics at Princeton University in the Mechanical and Aerospace Engineering Department, where he also serves as the director of Princeton's Electric Propulsion and Plasma Dynamics Laboratory and the 3D Audio and

Applied Acoustics (3D3A) Lab. As part of his work at the 3D3A Lab, he has generated several groundbreaking patents, including a new technique for producing tonally pure three-dimensional sound that is currently used in consumer audio products.

JEFF DOLVEN is a scholar, critic, and poet who continually jumps the fence between academic and creative work. He is professor in the English Department at Princeton University. His most recent book is *Senses of Style: Poetry before Interpretation*. His poetry collection is *Speculative Music*.

GUSTAVO DUDAMEL, Music and Artistic Director of the Los Angeles Philharmonic, has devoted his internationally celebrated conducting career to advocating for arts education as a means to a more just, peaceful, and integrated society. His contribution to this volume extends from a multifaceted residency at Princeton University Concerts during the series' 125th anniversary.

EDWARD DUSINBERRE, first violinist of the GRAMMY Award-winning Takács Quartet, has as distinct a voice as an author as he does as a musician. Always compelled to blur the boundary between performer and audience, his book *Beethoven for a Later Age: The Journey of a String Quartet* takes readers behind the scenes into the life of a professional string quartet.

CORINNA DA FONSECA-WOLLHEIM is celebrated for the directness and humanity with which she approaches music criticism as a contributing writer for the *New York Times*. She considers the act of listening to be its own art form—one which, when harnessed, reaches far beyond the walls of the concert hall.

FRANK GEHRY approaches his groundbreaking and playful architectural designs, including the Guggenheim Museum Bilbao, with the same narrative expressivity that he finds in music. Drawn to the interchange between music and architecture, in recent years he has designed several concert halls, including the Pierre Boulez Saal (Berlin) and Walt Disney Concert Hall (Los Angeles). His passion for music is shared by his friend MARK SWED, chief music critic for the *Los Angeles Times*, who has been a pillar of contemporary criticism since joining the newspaper's staff in 1996. A finalist for the Pulitzer Prize in criticism, his ardent writing, renowned for its ability to bring music to life, has appeared in sources as diverse as the best-selling iPad app *The Orchestra*, as well as in the most prestigious publications across the country and overseas.

RUTH BADER GINSBURG (1933–2020) was a Supreme Court Justice and one of history's greatest legal minds, as well as a champion of women's rights—and of classical music. She was a frequent attendee of the Washington Opera, where she on occasion made cameo appearances in productions. For Justice Ginsburg, instilling this passion for music in her children was of paramount importance. Her son, JAMES GINSBURG, upholds this passion to this day as a GRAMMY-nominated classical music producer. He is the president of Cedille Records, a record label that he founded while a law student at the University of Chicago. NINA TOTENBERG's coverage of the Supreme Court, as NPR's award-winning legal affairs correspondent, led to an enduring close friendship with Justice Ginsburg and her family. MELISSA LANE writes, speaks, and teaches about the meaning and value of constitutionalism, office, and law in ancient Greek political thought and practice, drawing out its relevance for the challenges of today. A professor at Princeton University, she is also engaged in musical and artistic communities in both the United States and the United Kingdom.

JANE HIRSHFIELD is one of American poetry's central spokespersons for concerns of the biosphere. Her poems, essays, and translations are devoted to the heightening of awareness and attention and to the recognition of interconnection, between disciplines, cultures, eras, and beings. A former Chancellor of the Academy of American Poets, she is the author of nine collections of poetry, including *Ledger* (2020); *The Beauty* (2015), long-listed for the National Book Award; and *Given Sugar, Given Salt* (2001), a finalist for the National Book Critics Circle Award. Other honors include fellowships from the Guggenheim and Rockefeller foundations and the National Endowment for the Arts. In 2019, she was elected into the American Academy of Arts & Sciences.

PICO IYER has made his eloquent and incisive inquiries into our interconnected world accessible to millions through a prolific and broad career as a travel writer, novelist, essayist, and TED speaker. His awareness of music's integral role in developing our global culture is reflected in his own contributions to liner and program notes, as well as a libretto for a narrative work written for the Auckland Chamber Orchestra.

ALEXANDER KLUGE is one of Germany's preeminent public intellectuals as well as a writer and filmmaker of international renown, with an abiding interest in music, opera in particular. Known for his radical innovations in both literary and cinematic form and for his collaborations, he brings the historical record to bear on our contemporary moment. His most recent books translated into English include *Temple of the Scapegoat: Opera Stories* and *Parsifal Container* (with Georg Baselitz).

NATHANIEL MACKEY approaches his award-winning poetry keenly aware of the musicality of language. Having spent some thirty years as a radio DJ, he imbues his poems with the rhythms and spirit of the music he loves. He recently served as the Chancellor of The Academy of American Poets, and he is also the recipient of the Poetry Foundation's Ruth Lilly Prize, a Guggenheim Fellowship, the National Book Award, and the Bollingen Prize.

MAUREEN N. MCLANE is a celebrated poet, critic, and professor of English at New York University. Her book *My Poets* is a hybrid of memoir and criticism that is as free in its formal inventions and as intimate in its narrative voice as are her own acclaimed poetry collections, which include *World Enough*, *Some Say*, and *Mz N: the serial*, among others.

ALICIA HALL MORAN and her husband, JASON MORAN, have focused much of their two-decade-long artistic partnership on projects that give voice to ignored and misrepresented aspects of their vibrant cultural background. The substance of this work blurs the boundaries of genre, though both artists are leaders in their distinct fields: Alicia is a classically trained mezzo-soprano who has also starred on Broadway, recorded with Carrie Mae Weems and Bill T. Jones, and staged modern operas; Jason has redefined twenty-first-century jazz as a pianist, composer, performance artist, and MacArthur Fellow.

PAUL MULDOON is a Pulitzer Prize–winning poet, Princeton University professor, editor, critic, playwright, and translator, for whom song and poetry are inseparable. He has written libretti for opera, published several collections of lyrics, and realized his lifelong love of pop and rock music by forming his own band, the Rogue Oliphant, which plays original songs with accompanied spoken-word lyrics.

ELAINE PAGELS's ability to make her renowned study of religion accessible and relevant to millions of people through her books—including National Book Award winner *The Gnostic Gospels* and, most recently, best-seller *Why Religion?*—is emblematic of her talent for tapping into our humanity. The Princeton University Professor and National Humanities Medal recipient has often spoken of music's profound role within this collective consciousness.

ROBERT PINSKY has breathed new life into the role that poetry plays within our culture through numerous prize-winning anthologies, popular online lectures and national poetry initiatives, and collaborations with jazz and classical musicians. The former United States Poet Laureate has also written a landmark best-selling translation of Dante's *Inferno*, and he composed the libretto for Tod Machover's opera *Death and the Powers: A Robot Pageant*.

RICHARD POWERS's virtuosity weaving together science, art, and politics in his novels stems from his background as a former physicist, self-taught computer programmer, and amateur musician and composer. Music plays a central role in several of his books, including *The Time of Our Singing, The Gold Bug Variations,* and *Orfeo*. His novel *The Overstory* won the 2019 Pulitzer Prize in Fiction.

BRIAN SEIBERT has devoted his writing career to contextualizing dance as a critic for *The New York Times* and contributor to *The*

New Yorker. His passion, however, lies within the *sound* of dance—specifically, of tap dance. His book *What the Eye Hears* is the first authoritative history of tap dance, and was a finalist for the National Book Critics Circle Award in Nonfiction.

ARNOLD STEINHARDT's experience traveling the world for forty-five years as founding member and first violinist of the Guarneri Quartet has made him as beloved a storyteller as he is a musician. Fascinated by all that the nature of being a musician entails, he has written two books—*Indivisible by Four* and *Violin Dreams*—and keeps a monthly blog, "In the Key of Strawberry." SCOTT BURNHAM, too, continues to be enthralled by the ineffable power of music after a long career as one of the most preeminent musicologists of our time. Having published nearly fifty articles and three books, most of which focus on the music of Mozart, Beethoven, and Schubert, his writings and scholarship continue to prioritize the mesmerizing beauty and profound role of music within our lives. He currently teaches at the City University of New York, and is an Emeritus Professor at Princeton University.

SUSAN STEWART, Avalon Foundation University Professor in the Humanities at Princeton, has long explored music and sound as a poet, translator, and scholar. Her newest books are *Cinder: New and Selected Poems* and *The Ruins Lesson*. She has collaborated with the jazz composer and clarinetist Ben Goldberg, the composer Eliza Brown, the Network for New Music, and the Philadelphia Chamber Music Society. The composer James Primosch (1956–2021) set many of her lyrics, and they collaborated for decades on new sequences for baritone, soprano, and full choir. Their most recent song cycles were commissioned and performed by the Chicago Symphony, Bard's Longy School of Music, and the New Juilliard Ensemble.

ABIGAIL WASHBURN is as comfortable within the field of Chinese law as she is touring the world as a GRAMMY Award–winning vocalist, songwriter, and clawhammer banjo player. The combination of these passions has garnered her a reputation as an unofficial musical ambassador to China with a singular talent for creating inventive cross-cultural syntheses across seemingly disparate folk traditions, including projects with collaborator Wu Fei. She is also a TED Fellow, the first US-China Fellow at Vanderbilt University, and an Andrew W. Mellon DisTIL Fellow at UNC–Chapel Hill.

CARRIE MAE WEEMS, by shaping an extraordinary artistic language that blends photography, text, and audio and video work, has created some of the most definitive and deliberate portraits of our contemporary social identity. As a preeminent American artist, she was the first African American woman to have a retrospective at the Guggenheim Museum, and she has participated in exhibitions at major museums around the world.

SUSAN WHEELER is an award-winning poet and novelist. Her ear for the sounds, rhythms, and images of contemporary culture informs much of her work, including her jazz-inspired novel, *Record Palace*. She is the author of six books of poetry, and her work has appeared in *The New Yorker, The New York Times,* and *The Paris Review*, as well as in numerous editions of *The Best American Poetry*.

C.K. WILLIAMS (1936–2015) was a poet, critic, translator, and Princeton University professor whose work responded to war, politics, and injustice and brought awareness to the music of everyday life. His writing was recognized by almost every major poetry award, including the Pulitzer Prize and National Book Award. A lifelong lover of classical music, he developed a collaboration with pianist Richard Goode in his later years.

WU FEI is one of the world's foremost masters of the guzheng, a 21-string Chinese zither that she has transformed from a relic of ancient classicism into a genre-bending contemporary instrument. The Beijing-born, Nashville-based performer, composer, and improviser has fused Western and Chinese musical idioms into a new, cosmopolitan voice that has captivated sold-out audiences around the world. She shares her passion for building transcultural musical bridges with longtime collaborator Abigail Washburn.

Index